Bible 400
Teacher's Guide

CONTENTS

Curriculum Overview 3

LIFEPAC® Management 11

Teacher Notes 25

Alternate Tests 45

Answer Keys 69

Self Test Keys 103

Test Keys 127

Alternate Test Keys 137

Author: **Alpha Omega Staff**

Editor: Alan Christopherson, M.S.

Alpha Omega Publications®

804 N. 2nd Ave. E., Rock Rapids, IA 51246-1759
© MCMXCVII by Alpha Omega Publications, Inc.   All rights reserved.
LIFEPAC is a registered trademark of Alpha Omega Publications, Inc.

OVERVIEW

BIBLE

Curriculum Overview
Grades 1–12

Bible LIFEPAC Overview

	Grade 1	Grade 2	Grade 3
LIFEPAC 1	GOD CREATED ALL THINGS • God created day and night • God created land and sea • God created plants and animals • God created people	WHO AM I? • God made us • God loves me • God helps me • God helped Daniel	WHY AM I HERE? • I love and obey God • I praise God • I worship God • I serve God
LIFEPAC 2	GOD LOVES HIS CHILDREN • God cared for Shadrach, Meshach, and Abednego • God cared for Joash and Esther • God cares for his Children • God's children love Him	THE STORY OF MOSES • The early life of Moses • Life in Midian • Moses returns to Egypt • Life in the desert	THE LIFE OF JESUS • Mary and Joseph • Jesus in the Temple • Jesus teaches and saves • Jesus dies and lives again
LIFEPAC 3	WE CAN PRAY • We can ask and thank God • We can pray God's special prayer • God listens to us • We listen to God	GOD AND YOU • God is great • God keeps his promises • You should obey God • God rewards his people	GOD'S PLAN FOR JOSEPH • The dream of Joseph • Joseph and his brothers • Joseph in Egypt • God watched over Joseph
LIFEPAC 4	GOD WANTS YOU TO BE GOOD • Jesus says love God • God says to love others • You show your love • God says to love yourself	HOW THE BIBLE CAME TO YOU • Moses and the Prophets • David and Solomon • The Apostles and Paul • Bible translators	YOU CAN USE THE BIBLE • The books of the Bible • How to read and study the Bible • How to find verses • How to memorize verses
LIFEPAC 5	OLD TESTAMENT STORIES • Joseph, Elijah, Jonathan, and David • Miriam and Deborah • A rich woman and her son • Ishmael and Mephibosheth	DAVID'S SLING • David with the sheep • David and the prophet • David and Saul • David and the giant	GOD CARES FOR HIS PEOPLE • God's love for people • God guides people • God protects people • God blesses people
LIFEPAC 6	GOD'S PROMISE • God's Old Testament promises • God's promises kept • The birth of the Promised One • The life of the Promised One	GOD IS EVERYWHERE • Understanding the beginning • Understanding God • The creation • God's will	THE BIBLE IS GOD'S WORD • The writers of God's Word • God's Word is preserved • God's Word changes lives • Promises of God's Word
LIFEPAC 7	JESUS, OUR SAVIOR • Jesus taught the people • Jesus healed the people • Jesus saves the people • Jesus will come again	THE STORY OF JOSEPH • Joseph as a boy at home • The worship of Joseph • Joseph in Egypt • Joseph and the famine	ARCHEOLOGY AND THE BIBLE • The search for treasure • Clues from old stories • Explaining the puzzles • Joining the search
LIFEPAC 8	GOD CALLS MISSIONARIES • The woman at the well • Stephen and Paul • Missionaries today • God calls missionaries	GOD AND THE FAMILY • The first family • Abraham's family • Happy families • God's promise to children	THE NEED FOR FRIENDS • We need love • We need friendship • God commands our love • Love for others
LIFEPAC 9	NEW TESTAMENT STORIES • Lazarus, Thomas, Stephen • Mary, Anna, Lydia • Children in the New Testament • Jesus and the children	GOD MADE THE NATIONS • The people of Babel • God's judgement at Babel • The new nation • Our big world	GOD'S PEOPLE HELP OTHERS • All people are created by God • God loves me • God's love to others • God is my Father
LIFEPAC 10	GOD GAVE YOU MANY GIFTS • God created all things • God loves His children • God gave us His Word • God gave us His Son	GOD, HIS WORD, AND YOU • God as our father • The word of God • Life with God • Belonging to God	GOD'S WORD, JESUS, AND YOU • God speaks to Man • Writers of the Word • Jesus and the Word • God's family

Grade 4	Grade 5	Grade 6	
HOW CAN I LIVE FOR GOD? • Peter found Jesus • Peter fished for Men • To be born into God's family • To be fruitful through the Spirit	**HOW OTHERS LIVED FOR GOD** • Fellow-laborers with God • Abraham, a man of faith • Servants of God • Co-workers with God	**FROM CREATION TO MOSES** • Creation • The Flood • Abraham and his descendants • Moses and the Law	LIFEPAC 1
GOD'S KNOWLEDGE • Knowledge to create • Learning God's knowledge • The benefits of God's knowledge • Using God's knowledge	**ANGELS** • Characteristics of Angels • Kinds of Angels • The ministry of Angels • Angels in the life of Jesus	**FROM JOSHUA TO SAMUEL** • Conquest and division of the land • The death of Joshua • The Judges of Israel • Ruth, Naomi, and Boaz	LIFEPAC 2
SAUL BEGINS TO LIVE FOR GOD • Saul persecutes the Christians • God changes Saul • Saul preaches about Jesus • Paul belongs to Christ	**THE PRESENCE OF GOD** • Everywhere as God • Everywhere as a person • In the lives of people • In my life	**THE KINGDOM OF ISRAEL** • Samuel and Saul • The reign of David • The reign of Solomon • The books of poetry	LIFEPAC 3
THE BIBLE AND ME • Reading and learning the Bible • Thinking about the Bible • Memorizing the Bible • Living the Bible way	**BIBLE METHODS AND STRUCTURE** • One book with many parts • Books of history • Books of poetry and prophecy • Books of the New Testament	**THE DIVIDED KINGDOM** • From Jeroboam to Captivity • Prophets of Judah and Israel • From Hezekiah to Captivity • Prophets of remaining kingdom	LIFEPAC 4
GOD CARES FOR US • The Twenty-third Psalm • Jesus and the sheep • David as a shepherd • Daniel as a helper	**THE CHRISTIAN IN THE WORLD** • Instruction and correction • Learning correct behavior • Relationships at school • Relationships in the world	**CAPTIVITY AND RESTORATION** • The prophets of the captivity • The returns from exile • The prophets of the Restoration • Creation to Restoration	LIFEPAC 5
HOW CAN I KNOW GOD EXISTS • God's plan for the Jews • A Jewish Savior • Man searches for God • Man needs God	**PROVING WHAT WE BELIEVE** • The Bible is God's Word • Evidence from the Bible • Evidence from history and science • Knowing that Christ arose	**THE LIFE OF JESUS** • Birth and background • The first years of ministry • The latter years of ministry • The death and Resurrection	LIFEPAC 6
OLD TESTAMENT GEOGRAPHY • Bible Geography • Description of the Land • Abram's Nomadic Life • Abraham's Descendants	**MISSIONARY JOURNEYS OF PAUL** • Paul's background • Paul's missionary journeys • The Jerusalem Council • Paul's last years	**THE FOLLOWERS OF JESUS** • The disciples of Jesus • The friends of Jesus • Miracles of Jesus • The message of Jesus	LIFEPAC 7
GOD–GIVEN WORTH • Who Am I? • God is my Creator • God is my Father • Knowing God's Love	**GOD CREATED MAN FOR ETERNITY** • Preparing for eternity • Christ is our Judge • The judgment of the Christian • The judgment of the unsaved	**THE APOSTLE PAUL** • Paul's background and conversion • Paul's missionary journeys • Paul's letters to churches • Paul's letters to people	LIFEPAC 8
WITNESSING FOR JESUS • Loving God and Others • Following Jesus • Knowing who Jesus is • Following Paul's Example	**AUTHORITY AND LAW** • God is the source of law • The model of law • The authority of the family • Our authority of government	**HEBREWS AND GENERAL EPISTLES** • The book of Hebrews • James and 1st and 2nd Peter • The three Johns • The book of Jude	LIFEPAC 9
GOD'S WAY IS PERFECT • Seeking Knowledge • Science & Geography • Living God's Way • Loving God's Way	**ANGELS, THE BIBLE, LIVING FOR GOD** • Presence of God and Angels • Understanding the Bible • Areas of service • The order of authority	**REVELATION AND REVIEW** • The Lord Jesus in Revelation • End-time events • Old Testament review • New Testament review	LIFEPAC 10

Bible LIFEPAC Overview

	Grade 7	Grade 8	Grade 9
LIFEPAC 1	**WORSHIP** • The nature of worship • Old Testament worship • New Testament worship • True worship	**PRAYER** • Organization of the Lord's Prayer • Purpose of the Lord's Prayer • History of prayer • Practical use of prayer	**THE NEW TESTAMENT** • Inter-Testamental period • Pharisees and Sadduces • New Testament themes • New Testament events
LIFEPAC 2	**MANKIND** • The origin of man • The fall of man • The re-creation of man • The mission of man	**SIN AND SALVATION** • The nature of sin • The need for salvation • How to receive salvation • The results of salvation	**THE GOSPELS** • Matthew • Mark • Luke • John
LIFEPAC 3	**THE ATTRIBUTES OF GOD** • God's nature of love • God's expression of love • The mercy of God • The grace of God	**ATTRIBUTES OF GOD** • God's justice • God's immutability • God's eternal nature • God's love	**THE ACTS OF THE APOSTLES** • The writer • The purpose • Pentecost • Missions
LIFEPAC 4	**FULFILLED PROPHECIES OF CHRIST** • Method of the First Advent • Purpose of the First Advent • The Messiah foretold • Fulfillment of the Messiah	**EARLY CHURCH LEADERS** • The early church • The church of the Middle Ages • The Renaissance • The Reformation	**THE PAULINE EPISTLES** • Paul as a person • The early epistles • Prison epistles • The later epistles
LIFEPAC 5	**LIVING THE BALANCED LIFE** • The Father's gift of life • Man's deception • Fellowship with the Savior • The life of the Spirit	**EARLY CHURCH HISTORY** • The Roman Empire • The background of the Jews • The ministry of Jesus • The Jerusalem church	**GENERAL EPISTLES** • James • First and Second Peter • First, Second, and Third John • Hebrews and Jude
LIFEPAC 6	**THE PSALMS** • The history of the Psalms • Types of Psalms • Hebrew poetry • Psalm 100	**THE EARLY CHURCHES** • The church at Antioch • The missionary journeys • The Jerusalem Conference • New Testament churches	**THE REVELATION OF JESUS CHRIST** • The seven churches • The seven seals and trumpets • The seven signs and plagues • The seven judgments and wonders
LIFEPAC 7	**THE LIFE OF CHRIST: PART ONE** • Early life of Christ • Christ's ministry begins • The early Judean ministry • The early Galilean ministry	**THE BOOK OF PROVERBS** • Literary forms and outline • Objectives and purposes • Influence on the New Testament • Key themes	**JOB AND SUFFERING** • The scenes of Job • Attitudes toward suffering • Christ's suffering on earth • The victory of Christ's suffering
LIFEPAC 8	**THE LIFE OF CHRIST: PART TWO** • The public ministry in Galilee • The private ministry in Galilee • The Judean ministry • The Perean ministry	**TODAY'S PROBLEMS** • Guidance for behavior • Characteristics of friendship • Studying effectively • Finding God's will	**HOW TO SHARE CHRIST** • Personal evangelism • Outreach to others • Personal and family missions • Assisting a missionary
LIFEPAC 9	**THE LIFE OF CHRIST: PART THREE** • The public Jerusalem ministry • The private Jerusalem ministry • The Crucifixion • The Resurrection	**UNDERSTANDING PARENTS** • Human parents • Biblical parents • Children's responsibility • Parents and children as a team	**GOD'S WILL FOR MY LIFE** • The desire of the heart • The Word and work of God • Importance of goals • The use of talents
LIFEPAC 10	**IN SUMMARY** • The plan of God • Man's history • The Savior's solution • Worship of Christ	**WALKING WITH GOD** • Prayer and salvation • The attributes of God • The early church leaders • Christian living	**THE WALK WITH CHRIST** • Background of the New Testament • The Epistles and Revelation • The importance of suffering • God's will for my life

Grade 10	Grade 11	Grade 12	
CREATION TO ABRAHAM • The six days of creation • The fall of man • Noah and his descendants • Nations of the earth	**THE FAITHFULNESS OF GOD** • Affirmation of God's faithfulness • Nature of God's faithfulness • Manifestations of God's faithfulness • Implications of God's faithfulness	**KNOWING YOURSELF** • Your creation by God • Interacting with others • A child and servant of God • Your personal skills	LIFEPAC 1
ABRAHAM TO MOSES • Abraham's call and promise • The covenant with Isaac • The life of Jacob • Joseph and his family	**ROMANS: PART ONE** • The Roman Empire and Church • The book of Romans • Paul's message to the Romans • Sin and salvation in Romans	**CHRISTIAN MINISTRIES** • Christian ministry defined • Church related ministries • Other ministries • A ministry as a career	LIFEPAC 2
EXODUS AND WANDERINGS • The journey to Sinai • The giving of the Law • Numbering the people • The book of Deuteronomy	**ROMANS: PART TWO** • The chosen of God • Service and submission • From sin to salvation • The victory of salvation	**CHOOSING A CHRISTIAN MINISTRY** • Where to look for a ministry • What to look for in a ministry • How to look for a ministry • Choosing a ministry for a career	LIFEPAC 3
ISRAEL IN CANAAN • Preparing for battle • The fight for the land • Dividing the land • The death of Joshua	**THE DOCTRINE OF JESUS CHRIST** • Identity and incarnation of Christ • The individuality of Christ • Christ's work on the Cross • Christ's work after the Cross	**GODHEAD** • Old Testament view • New Testament view • Historical Perspectives • Faith and man's relationship	LIFEPAC 4
THE JUDGES AND SPIRITUAL DECLINE • Background of Judges • History of the Judges • Examples of spiritual decay • Ruth and redemption	**THE NATION OF ISRAEL** • The covenant with Abraham • Israel as a nation • Old Testament archaeology • New Testament archaeology	**ATTRIBUTES OF GOD** • The Holiness of God • The Goodness of God • Holiness and the believer • Goodness and the Creation	LIFEPAC 5
THE KINGDOM • Samuel and Saul • David • Solomon • Hebrew poetry	**HISTORY OF THE CANON** • Revelation and inspiration • Illumination and interpretation • Authority of the Bible • Formation of the Bible	**THE EPISTLES OF JAMES** • James the man • The message of James • John the man • The message of John's epistles	LIFEPAC 6
THE DIVIDED KINGDOM • Jeroboam to Ahab • Ahab to Jehu • Jehu to Assyrian captivity • Prophets of the period	**FRIENDSHIP, DATING, AND MARRIAGE** • Meaning and role of friendship • Perspectives of dating • Principles of relationships • The structure of marriage	**DANIEL** • A man of conviction • An interpreter of dreams • A watchman in prayer • A man of visions	LIFEPAC 7
THE REMAINING KINGDOM • The time of Hezekiah • Manasseh to Josiah • Jehoahaz to the exile • Prophets of the period	**THE PURSUIT OF HAPPINESS** • Solomon's succession • Solomon's prosperity • Solomon's fall • Solomon's reflections	**COMPARATIVE RELIGIONS** • Elements of Christianity • The validity of Christian faith • World religions • The occult	LIFEPAC 8
THE CAPTIVITY • Prophets of the period • Jeremiah • Ezekiel • Daniel	**ANSWERS FOR AGNOSTICS** • Integrity of the Bible • Doctrines of the Bible • Interpretation of the Bible • Application of the Bible	**WISDOM FOR TODAY'S YOUTH** • Life and character of David • Life and riches of Solomon • Psalms and Proverbs • The Bible and literature	LIFEPAC 9
THE RESTORATION • First return from exile • The Jews preserved • Second return from exile • Haggai, Zechariah, and Malachi	**GOD, HIS WORD, AND THE CHRISTIAN** • The uniqueness of the Bible • History of Israel • God revealed in the Bible • Principles for living	**PRACTICAL CHRISTIAN LIVING** • Christian fundamentals • Growing in Christian maturity • A ministry for Christ • A testimony for Christ	LIFEPAC 10

MANAGEMENT

STRUCTURE OF THE LIFEPAC CURRICULUM

The LIFEPAC curriculum is conveniently structured to provide one teacher handbook containing teacher support material with answer keys and ten student worktexts for each subject at grade levels two through twelve. The worktext format of the LIFEPACs allows the student to read the textual information and complete workbook activities all in the same booklet. The easy to follow LIFEPAC numbering system lists the grade as the first number(s) and the last two digits as the number of the series. For example, the Language Arts LIFEPAC at the 6th grade level, 5th book in the series would be LAN0605.

Each LIFEPAC is divided into 3 to 5 sections and begins with an introduction or overview of the booklet as well as a series of specific learning objectives to give a purpose to the study of the LIFEPAC. The introduction and objectives are followed by a vocabulary section which may be found at the beginning of each section at the lower levels, at the beginning of the LIFEPAC in the middle grades, or in the glossary at the high school level. Vocabulary words are used to develop word recognition and should not be confused with the spelling words introduced later in the LIFEPAC. The student should learn all vocabulary words before working the LIFEPAC sections to improve comprehension, retention, and reading skills.

Each activity or written assignment has a number for easy identification, such as 1.1. The first number corresponds to the LIFEPAC section and the number to the right of the decimal is the number of the activity.

Teacher checkpoints, which are essential to maintain quality learning, are found at various locations throughout the LIFEPAC. The teacher should check 1) neatness of work and penmanship, 2) quality of understanding (tested with a short oral quiz), 3) thoroughness of answers (complete sentences and paragraphs, correct spelling, etc.), 4) completion of activities (no blank spaces), and 5) accuracy of answers as compared to the answer key (all answers correct).

The self test questions are also number coded for easy reference. For example, 2.015 means that this is the 15th question in the self test of Section II. The first number corresponds to the LIFEPAC section, the zero indicates that it is a self test question, and the number to the right of the zero the question number.

The LIFEPAC test is packaged at the centerfold of each LIFEPAC. It should be removed and put aside before giving the booklet to the student for study.

Answer and test keys have the same numbering system as the LIFEPACs and appear at the back of this handbook. The student may be given access to the answer keys (not the test keys) under teacher supervision so that he can score his own work.

A thorough study of the Curriculum Overview by the teacher before instruction begins is essential to the success of the student. The teacher should become familiar with expected skill mastery and understand how these grade level skills fit into the overall skill development of the curriculum. The teacher should also preview the objectives that appear at the beginning of each LIFEPAC for additional preparation and planning.

TEST SCORING and GRADING

Answer keys and test keys give examples of correct answers. They convey the idea, but the student may use many ways to express a correct answer. The teacher should check for the essence of the answer, not for the exact wording. Many questions are high level and require thinking and creativity on the part of the student. Each answer should be scored based on whether or not the main idea written by the student matches the model example. "Any Order" or "Either Order" in a key indicates that no particular order is necessary to be correct.

Most self tests and LIFEPAC tests at the lower elementary levels are scored at 1 point per answer; however, the upper levels may have a point system awarding 2 to 5 points for various answers or questions. Further, the total test points will vary; they may not always equal 100 points. They may be 78, 85, 100, 105, etc.

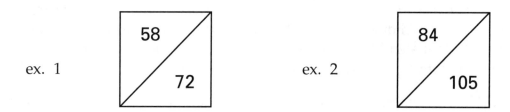

A score box similar to ex.1 above is located at the end of each self test and on the front of the LIFEPAC test. The bottom score, 72, represents the total number of points possible on the test. The upper score, 58, represents the number of points your student will need to receive an 80% or passing grade. If you wish to establish the exact percentage that your student has achieved, find the total points of his correct answers and divide it by the bottom number (in this case 72.) For example, if your student has a point total of 65, divide 65 by 72 for a grade of 90%. Referring to ex. 2, on a test with a total of 105 possible points, the student would have to receive a minimum of 84 correct points for an 80% or passing grade. If your student has received 93 points, simply divide the 93 by 105 for a percentage grade of 89%. Students who receive a score below 80% should review the LIFEPAC and retest using the appropriate Alternate Test found in the Teacher's Guide.

The following is a guideline to assign letter grades for completed LIFEPACs based on a maximum total score of 100 points.

LIFEPAC Test = 60% of the Total Score (or percent grade)
Self Test = 25% of the Total Score (average percent of self tests)
Reports = 10% or 10* points per LIFEPAC
Oral Work = 5% or 5* points per LIFEPAC
*Determined by the teacher's subjective evaluation of the student's daily work.

Example:

LIFEPAC Test Score	=	92%	92	x	.60		=	55 points
Self Test Average	=	90%	90	x	.25		=	23 points
Reports							=	8 points
Oral Work							=	4 points

TOTAL POINTS = 90 points

Grade Scale based on point system:

100	–	94	=	A
93	–	86	=	B
85	–	77	=	C
76	–	70	=	D
Below		70	=	F

TEACHER HINTS and STUDYING TECHNIQUES

LIFEPAC Activities are written to check the level of understanding of the preceding text. The student may look back to the text as necessary to complete these activities; however, a student should never attempt to do the activities without reading (studying) the text first. Self tests and LIFEPAC tests are never open book tests.

Language arts activities (skill integration) often appear within other subject curriculum. The purpose is to give the student an opportunity to test his skill mastery outside of the context in which it was presented.

Writing complete answers (paragraphs) to some questions is an integral part of the LIFEPAC Curriculum in all subjects. This builds communication and organization skills, increases understanding and retention of ideas, and helps enforce good penmanship. Complete sentences should be encouraged for this type of activity. Obviously, single words or phrases do not meet the intent of the activity, since multiple lines are given for the response.

Review is essential to student success. Time invested in review where review is suggested will be time saved in correcting errors later. Self tests, unlike the section activities, are closed book. This procedure helps to identify weaknesses before they become too great to overcome. Certain objectives from self tests are cumulative and test previous sections; therefore, good preparation for a self test must include all material studied up to that testing point.

The following procedure checklist has been found to be successful in developing good study habits in the LIFEPAC curriculum.

1. Read the introduction and Table of Contents.
2. Read the objectives.
3. Recite and study the entire vocabulary (glossary) list.
4. Study each section as follows:
    a. Read the introduction and study the section objectives.
    b. Read all the text for the entire section, but answer none of the activities.
    c. Return to the beginning of the section and memorize each vocabulary word and definition.
    d. Reread the section, complete the activities, check the answers with the answer key, correct all errors, and have the teacher check.
    e. Read the self test but do not answer the questions.
    f. Go to the beginning of the first section and reread the text and answers to the activities up to the self test you have not yet done.
    g. Answer the questions to the self test without looking back.
    h. Have the self test checked by the teacher.
    i. Correct the self test and have the teacher check the corrections.
    j. Repeat steps a–i for each section.

5. Use the SQ3R* method to prepare for the LIFEPAC test.
6. Take the LIFEPAC test as a closed book test.
7. LIFEPAC tests are administered and scored under direct teacher supervision. Students who receive scores below 80% should review the LIFEPAC using the SQ3R* study method and take the Alternate Test located in the Teacher Handbook. The final test grade may be the grade on the Alternate Test or an average of the grades from the original LIFEPAC test and the Alternate Test.

    *SQ3R: **S**can the whole LIFEPAC.

            Question yourself on the objectives.

            Read the whole LIFEPAC again.

            Recite through an oral examination.

            Review weak areas.

GOAL SETTING and SCHEDULES

Each school must develop its own schedule, because no single set of procedures will fit every situation. The following is an example of a daily schedule that includes the five LIFEPAC subjects as well as time slotted for special activities.

Possible Daily Schedule

8:15	–	8:25	Pledges, prayer, songs, devotions, etc.
8:25	–	9:10	Bible
9:10	–	9:55	Language Arts
9:55	–	10:15	Recess (juice break)
10:15	–	11:00	Mathematics
11:00	–	11:45	Social Studies
11:45	–	12:30	Lunch, recess, quiet time
12:30	–	1:15	Science
1:15	–		Drill, remedial work, enrichment*

*Enrichment: Computer time, physical education, field trips, fun reading, games and puzzles, family business, hobbies, resource persons, guests, crafts, creative work, electives, music appreciation, projects.

Basically, two factors need to be considered when assigning work to a student in the LIFEPAC curriculum.

The first is time. An average of 45 minutes should be devoted to each subject, each day. Remember, this is only an average. Because of extenuating circumstances a student may spend only 15 minutes on a subject one day and the next day spend 90 minutes on the same subject.

The second factor is the number of pages to be worked in each subject. A single LIFEPAC is designed to take 3 to 4 weeks to complete. Allowing about 3-4 days for LIFEPAC introduction, review, and tests, the student has approximately 15 days to complete the LIFEPAC pages. Simply take the number of pages in the LIFEPAC, divide it by 15 and you will have the number of pages that must be completed on a daily basis to keep the student on schedule. For example, a LIFEPAC containing 45 pages will require 3 completed pages per day. Again, this is only an average. While working a 45 page LIFEPAC, the student may complete only 1 page the first day if the text has a lot of activities or reports, but go on to complete 5 pages the next day.

Long range planning requires some organization. Because the traditional school year originates in the early fall of one year and continues to late spring of the following year, a calendar should be devised that covers this period of time. Approximate beginning and completion dates can be noted on the calendar as well as special occasions such as holidays, vacations and birthdays. Since each LIFEPAC takes 3-4 weeks or eighteen days to complete, it should take about 180 school days to finish a set of ten LIFEPACs. Starting at the beginning school date, mark off eighteen school days on the calendar and that will become the targeted completion date for the first LIFEPAC. Continue marking the calendar until you have established dates for the remaining nine LIFEPACs, making adjustments for previously noted holidays and vacations. If all five subjects are being used, the ten established target dates should be the same for the LIFEPACs in each subject.

FORMS

The sample weekly lesson plan and student grading sheet forms are included in this section as teacher support materials and may be duplicated at the convenience of the teacher.

The student grading sheet is provided for those who desire to follow the suggested guidelines for assignment of letter grades found on page 3 of this section. The student's self test scores should be posted as percentage grades. When the LIFEPAC is completed the teacher should average the self test grades, multiply the average by .25 and post the points in the box marked self test points. The LIFEPAC percentage grade should be multiplied by .60 and posted. Next, the teacher should award and post points for written reports and oral work. A report may be any type of written work assigned to the student whether it is a LIFEPAC or additional learning activity. Oral work includes the student's ability to respond orally to questions which may or may not be related to LIFEPAC activities or any type of oral report assigned by the teacher. The points may then be totaled and a final grade entered along with the date that the LIFEPAC was completed.

The Student Record Book which was specifically designed for use with the Alpha Omega curriculum provides space to record weekly progress for one student over a nine week period as well as a place to post self test and LIFEPAC scores. The Student Record Books are available through the current Alpha Omega catalog; however, unlike the enclosed forms these books are not for duplication and should be purchased in sets of four to cover a full academic year.

WEEKLY LESSON PLANNER

Week of:

	Subject	Subject	Subject	Subject
Monday				
	Subject	Subject	Subject	Subject
Tuesday				
	Subject	Subject	Subject	Subject
Wednesday				
	Subject	Subject	Subject	Subject
Thursday				
	Subject	Subject	Subject	Subject
Friday				

WEEKLY LESSON PLANNER

Week of:

	Subject	Subject	Subject	Subject
Monday				
	Subject	Subject	Subject	Subject
Tuesday				
	Subject	Subject	Subject	Subject
Wednesday				
	Subject	Subject	Subject	Subject
Thursday				
	Subject	Subject	Subject	Subject
Friday				

Student Name _____   Year _____

Bible

LP #	Self Test Scores by Sections 1	2	3	4	5	Self Test Points	LIFEPAC Test	Oral Points	Report Points	Final Grade	Date
01											
02											
03											
04											
05											
06											
07											
08											
09											
10											

History & Geography

LP #	Self Test Scores by Sections 1	2	3	4	5	Self Test Points	LIFEPAC Test	Oral Points	Report Points	Final Grade	Date
01											
02											
03											
04											
05											
06											
07											
08											
09											
10											

Language Arts

LP #	Self Test Scores by Sections 1	2	3	4	5	Self Test Points	LIFEPAC Test	Oral Points	Report Points	Final Grade	Date
01											
02											
03											
04											
05											
06											
07											
08											
09											
10											

Student Name _____   Year _____

Mathematics

LP #	Self Test Scores by Sections 1	2	3	4	5	Self Test Points	LIFEPAC Test	Oral Points	Report Points	Final Grade	Date
01											
02											
03											
04											
05											
06											
07											
08											
09											
10											

Science

LP #	Self Test Scores by Sections 1	2	3	4	5	Self Test Points	LIFEPAC Test	Oral Points	Report Points	Final Grade	Date
01											
02											
03											
04											
05											
06											
07											
08											
09											
10											

Spelling/Electives

LP #	Self Test Scores by Sections 1	2	3	4	5	Self Test Points	LIFEPAC Test	Oral Points	Report Points	Final Grade	Date
01											
02											
03											
04											
05											
06											
07											
08											
09											
10											

TEACHER

N
O
T
E
S

INSTRUCTIONS FOR BIBLE

The Alpha Omega Curriculum from grades two through twelve was written with the daily instructional material written directly in the LIFEPACs. The student is encouraged to read and follow his own instructional material, thus developing independent study habits. The teacher should introduce the LIFEPAC to the student, set a required completion schedule, complete teacher checks, be available for questions regarding both subject content and procedures, administer and grade tests, and develop additional learning activities as desired. Teachers working with several students may schedule their time so that students are assigned to a quiet work activity when it is necessary to spend instructional time with one particular student.

The Teacher Notes section of the handbook lists the required or suggested materials for the LIFEPACs and provides additional learning activities for the students. The materials section refers only to LIFEPAC materials and does not include materials which may be needed for the additional activities. Additional learning activities provide a change from the daily school routine, encourage the student's interest in learning, and may be used as a reward for good study habits.

Materials Needed for LIFEPAC

Required: Suggested:
Bible   none

Additional Learning Activities

Section I How Peter lived for God

1. Discuss these questions
   a. What was Linda and Leonard's class studying?
   b. Where had Linda's uncle been digging?
   c. What did Linda's uncle find?
   d. What did Linda's uncle pretend?
   e. What would Hali's diary have been written on?
   f. How did John introduce Jesus?
   g. How were lambs used?
   h. Who was Andrew's brother?
   i. What did Jesus call Simon?
   j. Does Jesus know your name?
   k. Does Jesus know your parents?
   l. What name did Jesus give Simon?
   m. What did the name *Peter* mean?
   n. What body of water is near the town of Bethsaida?
   o. What did Jesus tell Simon, Peter, and Andrew?
   p. What do you think "fishing for men" meant?
   q. Why did Peter obey Jesus?
   r. How did Jesus feed the crowd of five thousand?
   s. What did Jesus do when he went to the mountain?
   t. Who walked on the water?
   u. What happened when Peter took his eyes off Jesus?
   v. How many disciples did Jesus have?
   w. How many times did Peter think you should forgive someone?
   x. How many times did Jesus say you should forgive someone?
2. Have a student write a diary, like Hali's, that deals with a day with Jesus. Have the student describe the different things Jesus did: for example, healed the sick, taught, and so forth.
3. Have students make an oral or a written report on the events in Peter's life. List events before Pentecost and then after Pentecost and indicate how he had changed.

Section II How Can I Live for God

1. Discuss these questions
   a. Who was Nicodemus?
   b. What is the second birth?
   c. When are we born into God's family?
   d. What did God tell Moses to do to remove the serpents?
   e. What is our spiritual milk?
   f. How can we be a "doer" of God's Word?

g. What should we do when we sin?

h. Can you name the fruit of the spirit?

i. What is another word for patience?

j. What happens in heaven when one sinner repents?

k. What is the greatest joy for a Christian?

l. What should we do for those who don't know Christ?

m. What is a suffix?

2. Have the students think of synonyms for the fruit of the Spirit.

3. Have a student try to make a puzzle that includes the words *Nicodemus, disobeyed, Jesus, life,* and so on.

4. Make a scroll. Take one of the stories from this LIFEPAC and copy it on the scroll. Use your best handwriting.

5. Make a poster about the fruit of the Spirit.

Materials Needed for LIFEPAC

Required: Suggested:
Bible   none

Additional Learning Activities

Section I The Evidence of God's Knowledge

1. Discuss these questions
    a. How did God use His knowledge?
    b. What did the boy do before he planted his garden?
    c. How did the boy's name get in the garden?
    d. What did God leave to show us He created the world?
    e. How is God's knowledge different from our knowledge?
    f. How did God give man breath?
    g. Who did God give us to love us?
    h. How does God's knowledge help us?
    i. How can you count the number of syllables in a word?
    j. How did God create man?
2. The students may make a mural of pictures showing the days of Creation.
3. Write a poem on how it will be living with God forever (eternity).

Section II The Instruction of God's Knowledge

1. Discuss these questions
    a. Why was the Bible written?
    b. Whom did God choose to write the Bible?
    c. When did these men write the Bible?
    d. What does the Bible tell us about Jewish people?
    e. When did the Jewish people return to Israel?
    f. What will help us have stronger faith?
    g. What do you need to learn something well?
    h. Who helps us live for Jesus?
    i. Where do heavenly thoughts and desires come from?
    j. What will the Holy Spirit give us?
    k. What is the Holy Spirit?
    l. Who promised to send the Holy Spirit to help believers?
    m. What are some things we should do when we pray?
    n. What are some things we will do when we accept Christ?
2. Students could explain to each other which writer of the Bible they would like to meet and why.
3. Write a paragraph on why Jesus is a good teacher.

Section III The Benefits of God's Knowledge

1. Discuss these questions
    a. Does anyone ever live without doing wrong?
    b. How did God provide for our sins to be forgiven?
    c. Why is Jesus called the Lamb of God?
    d. Why did Jesus come to earth?
    e. What is God's plan for our lives?

  f. How does God correct us when we are wrong?

 2. The class may recite John 3:16 as a choral reading. The boys can do the first part and the girls the last.

 3. Write a paragraph on how life might be in heaven without any sin.

Section IV The Use of God's Knowledge

 1. Discuss these questions

  a. How does Jesus feel about children?

  b. Why is it important to find Jesus when you are young?

  c. What would be a wrong way to seek knowledge?

  d. Who was chosen by God to build a temple?

  e. What did Solomon want?

  f. How did God feel about Solomon's request?

  g. Where can we find some of Solomon's wise thoughts?

  h. What does a paragraph sometimes tell us about a word?

  i. What does God give everyone?

  j. How can we find out what God wants us to do?

 2. Students in pairs may help each other memorize the verses in Section IV of the LIFEPAC and recite them in front of the class.

 3. Write a paragraph on what you might want if God asked you (like Solomon's request for wisdom).

Materials Needed for LIFEPAC

Required:
Bible
encyclopedia or Internet access
10 pieces of cardboard
crayons
wide masking or mending tape
newsprint paper
markers
world atlas

Suggested:
Bible "costumes"
clay or salt dough
colored pencils
yarn
glitter
glue

Additional Learning Activities

Section I Saul Persecutes Christians

1. Write a skit to show Stephen's death. Perform it before the class.
2. Make a model of the city of Damascus in clay or salt dough as it was in New Testament times or as it is now.
3. Tell the story of Damascus, the oldest, continuously inhabited city in the world, by letting small groups contribute information for each historical period (Abraham, Paul, Crusades, today).
4. From an encyclopedia or an Internet search, find out how children learned to read and write in New Testament times.
5. Read about Luke and his writing the Acts of the Apostles. Add the story to your book of information about Bible authors.
6. Read about the modern city of Damascus.

   ✳ The following activities may be used for all sections of this LIFEPAC:

7. Write five sentences about the story. Make some true and some false. Exchange your questions with a partner and check each other's work.
8. Write three to five multiple choice questions about the story and quiz a classmate.
9. Write a paragraph that summarizes the story.
10. Allow the students to re-tell the story in his/her own words.
11. List the names of the important people in the Bible story. Write three words to describe each person.
12. Make flash cards using the vocabulary words and practice with them before each self test.
13. Write one synonym and one antonym for each vocabulary word.
14. Skim the story. List words that tell who, what, when, where, and how.
15. Play a form of "Jeopardy." You provide the answer; students must either write or say the correct question.

Sections II God Changes Saul's Plans

1. Make a tent as Paul might have made.
2. Act out events in Paul's life, especially in the journey to Damascus.
3. Make a model in salt dough or clay of a synagogue.

4. Write a letter to a friend in Jerusalem telling how the news of Saul's (Paul's) conversion was told in Damascus.

5. Find out about Tarsus, Paul's hometown, and add information to your own atlas.

6. Pretend that you were traveling with Paul. What did you see? What did you hear? What happened? Write about it.

Section III God Uses Saul

1. Find out about the cities to which Christians wrote letters.

2. Learn about Barnabas, Ananias, Gamaliel, Silas, Stephen, Luke, Timothy, Titus, and Lydia. Then, allow each student to choose his/her favorite character. One at a time, each student should impersonate his/her character. The other students may ask a series of questions to each character to try to guess who he/she is.

3. Find other verses from Paul's letters and memorize them, such as 1 Corinthians 13:13.

4. Take the picture sequence that was one of the activities in Section III to a class of younger children and tell the story of Paul for them using your pictures.

5. A Fish Pond Game may be made from the design provided.
   Instructions for playing Fish Pond: Write questions on the fish. Teacher or student has answers.
   Let each student fish for a question.
   If he answers questions, he may keep the fish.
   The one who has most fish at end of game is winner.

6. Divide the class into 13 groups and assign each group 1 of Paul's New Testament letters. (If the class is smaller—or for homeschoolers—have the students choose one of the letters.) Each group should answer the following questions for each letter:
   a. To whom was the letter written?
   b. When was the letter written?
   c. Who are the key people?
   d. What is the key place?
   e. What is a key verse contained in the letter?
   f. What is the theme of the letter? Compile all the information into a large class chart that can be displayed.

7. As a class, design a large map of Paul's missionary journeys. Include major cities and places where churches were established. Use different lines to indicate different journeys. The map may be as elaborate and detailed as you like.

8. Draw three pictures that show events from the beginning, middle, and end of the story of Paul. Write a sentence that describes each picture.

9. Make a word hunt or crossword puzzle using words from the story.

10. Make a large class book that tells the story of Paul. Allow the students to dictate as the teacher writes the story down on the pages. Allow the students to illustrate the book with markers, colored pencils, crayons, yarn, glitter, or any other materials as would be needed. (The pages may be laminated by machine or with clear contact paper if they are flat.) When completed, have the book spiral bound. Display it where the students may go back and re-read it.

Materials Needed for LIFEPAC

Required: Suggested:
Bible   none

Additional Learning Activities

Section I Studying the Bible

1. Small groups make up skits to show how to study the Bible. Other students see the finished skits and put the best ideas together for a class presentation to parents.
2. Choose pictures in magazines to illustrate people making wise choices. Place all pictures on a class bulletin board with the word WISDOM as the title.
3. Read the book of Proverbs in a modern translation.
4. Illustrate some Proverbs by making a diorama.
5. Illustrate a favorite Proverb with your own drawing.
6. Read other stories about Dwight L. Moody.

Section II Memorizing the Bible

1. Make a chart, using pictures from magazines, to show importance of memorizing verses from the Bible.
2. In small groups make up stories using proverbs as the morals.
3. Make a Bible Study Notebook using the time chart in Section II of the LIFEPAC as a model.
4. Make a mobile with the word PROVERBS. Hand illustrate verses from the book of Proverbs.

Section III Living the Bible Way

1. Using topics from the LIFEPAC, students may illustrate ideas by finding pictures from old magazines and mounting them on tagboard.
2. Follow topics listed in Section III, Living the Bible Way, and keep a diary of your prayers for better obedience.
3. Recite Proverbs learned at daily sharing time in the class and at home.

Materials Needed for LIFEPAC

Required:
Bible

Suggested:
none

Additional Learning Activities

Section I Christ Our Helper and Shepherd (Twenty-Third Psalm)

1. Recite the Twenty-Third Psalm as a group, in unison, and by two groups alternating verses.
2. Give personal testimonies of Jesus as the Good Shepherd.
3. Inquire of your parents and other adults of their experiences with God's care.
4. Write a psalm as a class.
5. As a field trip, visit a sheep ranch.
6. Use a filmstrip to show life on a sheep ranch.
7. Arrange for students to eat some food that David might have eaten (goats' milk, cheese, dates, figs, etc.).
8. Find verses in the New Testament where Jesus talks about shepherds and sheep and Himself as the Good Shepherd.
9. Make a chart to show the Psalms that David wrote.
10. Make a book of your favorite verses from Psalms by copying and illustrating.
11. Make a plan to increase your prayer life. Keep record of answered prayers.

Section II David the Shepherd

1. Dramatize the events in David's life. Each group may perform before the others.
2. Make bulletin board of students' illustrations of the events in David's life.
3. Make models of David and Goliath to show contrast in size and armor.
4. From the library or the Bible, get other stories about David and illustrate.
5. Select other people from the Bible and write a paragraph about each one to show how God used them.
6. Find out what David's sling looked like. Draw a picture of it.

Section III Daniel the Helper

1. Dramatize the events in Daniel's life with one group performing for the others.
2. Make a model in clay or salt dough of ancient Babylon.
3. Illustrate, by using pencil or crayon pictures, the events in Daniel's life.
4. Find examples of Babylonian writing (i.e. cunieform) and make up a code for a Bible verse using it.

Materials Needed for LIFEPAC

Required: Suggested:
none   Bible
                                       Bible dictionary
                                       encyclopedia
                                       clay
                                       salt dough
                                       tagboard or newsprint
                                       string, cardboard for mobile
                                       magazines
                                       ink pad

Additional Learning Activities

Section I God's Plan for People

1. Make models in clay of artifacts (cup, armor, beads, coins) from Ur.
2. Work in small groups to make a genealogical chart of Abraham and his descendants.
3. Find chart of the stars found in the sky above the Holy Land and make copy for mobile.
4. Find out the origins of these words:
   a. Hebrew
   b. Israelite
   c. Jew
   d. hallelujah.
5. Draw a map of Canaan in the time of Abraham.
6. Draw a map of Palestine in the time of Jesus.
7. Read the references in Matthew (2:6; 2:15; 2:18; and 2:23) and explain their meanings from the Old Testament.

Section II Man's Search for God

1. Make models of the planets in our galaxy. Size them in comparison to the sun.
2. Divide class into several groups. Let each group choose a category of things God has made (flowers, insects, animals, etc.) and find or draw pictures of as many as possible. Put the finished illustration on a bulletin board.
3. Find pictures of as many different people as possible to make a montage to illustrate the varieties of human beings.
4. Continue the study of the life of Thomas Aquinas.
5. Experiment with the understanding of great numbers (billion, trillion, etc.) by comparing sizes of various objects.
6. Read Psalm 8 and put the ideas found there into your own words.
7. Read further into the archaeological account of the fall of Jericho.
8. Choose a part of the body (eye, circulation system, skeleton) and read about its parts and functions. Draw a model.
9. Ask everyone to put his fingerprints on your paper. Check the differences.

Section III Man's Need of God

1. Find the poem "Each in His Own Tongue" By S. Caruthers and use it to explain man's need for God.

2. Find out about the authors of ten of the other books of the Bible (page 27 of LIFEPAC) and write a paragraph on each author.
3. Witness to friends and family your joy at having Jesus as your Savior.

Materials Needed for LIFEPAC

Required:
none

Suggested:
Bible
clay
salt dough
flatbed boxes
seeds

Additional Learning Activities

Section I Geography of the Old Testament

1. Make clay or salt dough model of the lands along the Fertile Crescent.
2. Make clay or salt dough model of Canaan.
3. Make model in salt dough or clay of modern irrigation systems such as found in California or Arizona.
4. Plant seeds in flatbed boxes to illustrate various ways to use watering systems. Use encyclopedias for information.
5. Find out about the climate in southwestern United States. Write a paragraph about it, comparing it with the climate in the Holy Land.
6. Find out about lands that depend on spring and fall rains to water crops (India, Pakistan, Australia, etc.). Make reports to the class.
7. Read about ways to climb mountains. Have small groups illustrate pictures of climbing equipment.
8. Write to California, Arizona, New Mexico, or other western states for information on desert survival.
9. Make displays of geographical terms for a bulletin board.

Section II Old Testament Men and Bible Lands

1. Make a model of the city of Ur.
2. Make a tent like those made by Abraham, Isaac, or Jacob.
3. Study the Nile River. Divide the class into small groups for reports on its sources, flooding, Aswan Dam, Abu Simbel, and so on. Let each group share its findings with the others.
4. Make paper from papyrus.
5. Make a coat for Joseph.
6. Find or make pictures of water wheels, *shaduf,* and irrigation canals for display.
7. Find out about the life of nomads in Abraham's time and modern days.
8. Read about the Dead Sea and the Sea of Galilee. Write a paragraph contrasting them.
9. Choose a plant mentioned in the Bible and see if you can grow one of your own.

Materials Needed for LIFEPAC

Required:	Suggested:
none	Bible
	book of Aesop's Fables
	record or cassette recording of
	"The Hallelujah Chorus" by
	Handel
	Bible dictionary
	encyclopedia
	filmstrip or mounted copies of
	"The Creation" by Michelangelo

Additional Learning Activities

Section I Who Am I?

1. Arrange for a small group to write a script telling the story of the tortoise and the hare. Let another group act it out for the class.
2. Show filmstrip or mounted copies of pictures of "The Creation" by Michelangelo and encourage students' expressions of appreciation of the masterpiece.
3. Find out other things about George Washington or Abraham Lincoln to show they were men of a humble heart.
4. Read more fables that point to a moral. Make a diorama to illustrate the morals.
5. Read other parables by Jesus to show contrast between the proud and the humble.
6. Read in an encyclopedia about sparrows and write a paragraph to show God's love of all creatures.

Section II God Is My Creator and My Father

1. Find a musical setting of Psalm 100 and learn it or make your own melody for the Psalm with the help of the teacher.
2. Make crossword puzzles from key words in Bible passages. Share the puzzles with other students.
3. Read Psalm 104, noting the examples of God's creative power. Draw a picture of each example and attach in sequence for picturization of the Psalm.
4. Listen to the "Hallelujah Chorus" by Handel for an awareness of the "King of Kings, Lord of Lords" setting.
5. Give examples of being created in God's image in an original poem or drawing.
6. Write a prayer of gratitude and of sorrow for sins. Share it aloud with a group at prayer time.

Section III How Does God Want Me to See Myself?

1. Make a list of questions and answers to help understand the importance of each child to God, His adoption of His children, His love for all, and what His children can do to glorify Him. Use questions and answers from *Knowing That God Loves Me* in Section III of the LIFEPAC.
2. Direct the acting out by a group of students of the story of David and Goliath.

3. Read in a book the ways your bodies and minds grow. Summarize in several paragraphs.

4. Make a list of the ways God takes care of you through other people. Under *A* , list needs; under *B* , list the people. Then find pictures to illustrate the list and make a bulletin board display. Example:

A	B
teaches you to understand the Bible	Sunday school teacher
cares for teeth	dentist

Materials Needed for LIFEPAC

Required: Suggested:
none   Bible
                    Bible dictionary
                    scrapbook pages
                    tagboard
                    crayons

Additional Learning Activities

Section I A Living Witness

1. Make up skits to illustrate ways to show God's love. Perform before class.
2. Visit a nursing home or hospital ward to cheer and comfort patients.
3. Act out events of Stephen's martyrdom before class.
4. Make a list of situations in which you have witnessed.
5. Write a hymn of praise and set it to the music of a familiar melody.
6. Write a prayer asking help with specific witness. Share with others.
7. Make a puzzle using guide words from the dictionary.
8. From the list of Jesus' activities in Section I of LIFEPAC, draw pictures to illustrate His "doing good."

Section II A Telling Witness

1. Encourage class members to contribute to a notebook, scrapbook, or bulletin board of information learned about customs or ways of living in Jesus' time.
2. Let class witness to each other and to adults. Encourage students to share experiences.
3. Draw a picture of Jesus and the two disciples at supper at Emmaus.
4. Find out from an encyclopedia about Samaria. Where was it? What was its capital? Why did the Jews have little to do with the people who lived there? What is the reason Jesus used a Samaritan as His example of a good neighbor?
5. Find out how the Roman Empire collected taxes. Write a paragraph for the class notebook.
6. Find out about the Pharisees. Write a paragraph for the class notebook.
7. Read 2 Corinthians 11:23–27. Make a list of Paul's sufferings for his telling the Good News.
8. Find out about Paul's Roman citizenship. How did he get it? What were the privileges? Write a paragraph for the class notebook.

Materials Needed for LIFEPAC

Required: Suggested:

none   Bible

Additional Learning Activities

Section I Learning God's Way

1. Make a relief map of the Holy Land.
2. Make a Holy Land village in a sand table.
3. Review the plan of salvation. Have students dramatize leading someone to the Lord.
4. Read about modern-day Christians being used by God.
5. Continually pray for people in need. List answers to prayer. Set up a prayer file.

ALTERNATE

TESTS

Reproducible Tests
for use with the Bible 400
Teacher's Guide

Name _____

Match these items (each answer, 2 points).

1.	_____	Uncle Gerald	a.	asked about forgiveness
2.	_____	Andrew	b.	archeologist
3.	_____	Bethsaida	c.	doesn't want any to perish
4.	_____	Jesus	d.	introduced Jesus
5.	_____	John	e.	made bronze serpent
6.	_____	Moses	f.	Peter's hometown
7.	_____	Nicodemus	g.	wrote in a diary
8.	_____	Holy Spirit	h.	produces fruit
9.	_____	the Lord	i.	ruler of the Jews
10.	_____	Peter	j.	Peter's brother
			k.	the Lamb of God

Answer these questions (each answer, 5 points).

11. What is faith?_____

_____

_____

12. What does *repent* mean?_____

_____

_____

Write *true* or *false* (each answer, 2 points).

13. _____ Jesus is called the Lamb of God because He can take away sin.

14. _____ Matthew brought Peter to Jesus.

15. _____ Jesus wanted His disciples to become fishers of men.

16. _____ Peter could not walk on the water because his faith was too little.

17. _____ Jesus told Nicodemus the story of Moses and the bronze serpent.

18. _____ Other people know you are Jesus' disciple because you say you are.

19. _____ God wants the good people to be saved and the bad people to perish.

20. _____ The first four fruits of the Spirit that are listed are love, joy, peace, and longsuffering.

21. _____ We must forgive people forty-nine times.

22. _____ Peter's hometown was Bethsaida.

Write the correct letter and answer on each line (each answer, 3 points).

23.   John called Jesus the_____.
        a. Lion of God b. Lamb of God   c. Crown of God

24.   Jesus called Peter and his brother to fish for_____.
        a. fish   b. whales   c. men

25.   Jesus washed the disciples'_____.
        a. feet   b. hands   c. faces

26.   Three thousand people repented when_____
        preached at Pentecost.
        a. Stephen   b. Peter   c. disciple

27.   Another name for one of the followers of Jesus is_____.
        a. Apostle   b. martyr   c. disciple

28.   Jesus taught that we should love_____.
        a. even our enemies
        b. only our relatives
        c. only those who love us

Complete these sentences (each answer, 4 points).

29.   Joy is in heaven when a sinner_____.

30.   When you sin, you should be sorry and ask God for_____.

31.   A Christian grows by reading and following God's_____.

32.   The first thing to do for a friend who needs to find Jesus is to
        _____ for the friend.

33.   Peter was brought to Jesus by his_____.

34.   After Jesus arose from the dead, He asked Peter to feed His
        _____.

35.   Hearing God's Word is not enough. We must also _____
        God's Word.

36.   If we forgive others, Jesus will also_____ us.

Date _____
Score _____
Possible Score _____ 100 _____

Name _____

Answer *true* or *false* (each answer, 2 points).
1. _____ God created the world in an orderly way.
2. _____ God wants us to live Christian lives.
3. _____ Some knowledge is not good for us.
4. _____ The Holy Spirit cannot help us.
5. _____ Prayer is speaking to God.
6. _____ Every person trusts Jesus as Savior.
7. _____ God does not hear us pray.
8. _____ Only God knows everything.
9. _____ God always loves us but He is sad when we sin.
10. _____ God does not have a plan for your life.

Write the correct letter and answer on each line (each answer, 2 points).
11. God is perfect in_____ .
    a. all ways
    b. only His knowledge
    c. heavenly ways
12. There are no mistakes in_____ .
    a. our lives   b. the Bible   c. man's knowledge
13. Jesus taught people that God_____ .
    a. only loves Christians
    b. cares about all their needs
    c. was going to create a world
14. Christian living means_____ .
    a. trying to do the ways of God
    b. becoming a preacher
    c. teaching Sunday School
15. God is *not* pleased with knowledge learned from_____ .
    a. Bible study
    b. star study
    c. teachers

Match these items (each answer, 3 points).

16. _____ Jesus
17. _____ the Bible
18. _____ Genesis
19. _____ righteousness
20. _____ disciple
21. _____ written without mistake
22. _____ created by God
23. _____ prays for us
24. _____ the Lamb of God
25. _____ sacrifice

a. follower
b. living in a way to please God
c. heaven
d. the Holy Spirit
e. Savior
f. Jesus
g. an offering to God
h. God's Word
i. the Bible
j. tells us that God created the world
k. the world

Complete these statements (each answer, 4 points).

26. God created the world in seven_____ .
27. The story of the Creation is found in the Bible in the book of_____ .
28. God made man from_____ .
29. God rested from His work on the_____ .
30. To *exist* means to_____ .
31. Jesus promised to send the_____ to us.
32. Matthew 28:19 tells us that "your_____ is the temple of the Holy Ghost."
33. The Bible says that God so loved the world that He gave His only_____ .
34. Solomon asked God for_____ .
35. The Bible says that the beginning of knowledge is_____ .

Date _____
Score _____
Possible Score _____ **100** _____

Name _____

Match these items (each answer, 3 points).

1. _____ This means to treat others badly or to punish them.

2. _____ This is a place where Jews gather for worship.

3. _____ This person studied Jewish law.

4. _____ This person is a follower of Jesus.

5. _____ He was Saul's teacher in Jerusalem.

6. _____ He was stoned for his faith in Jesus.

7. _____ He came to visit Saul in Damascus.

a. Ananias

b. Christian

c. Gamaliel

d. persecution

e. scribe

f. Stephen

g. synagogue

Place the events in the correct order. Write 1 beside what happened first, 2 beside what happened second, and so on (each answer, 3 points).

8. _____ Saul persecuted Christians.

9. _____ Saul was blind for three days.

10. _____ Saul learned to make tents.

11. _____ The Holy Spirit guided Saul in learning more about Jesus.

12. _____ Saul studied with Gamaliel.

13. _____ Saul saw a bright light on his way to Damascus.

14. _____ Saul traveled on many missionary journeys.

Circle the letter of the correct answer (each answer, 3 points).

15. The chief Jewish religious leader was known as the _____ .
    a. rabbi
    b. pastor
    c. high priest

16. A _____ was a Jewish religious teacher.
    a. rabbi
    b. pastor
    c. high priest

17. _____ believed in the resurrection of the dead and in angels.
    a. Sadducees
    b. Pharisees
    c. Rabbis

18. Saul held the _____ of those who stoned Stephen.
    a. robes
    b. hats
    c. sandals

19. Saul planned to travel from Jerusalem to _____ to persecute Christians.
     a. Tarsus   b. Rome   c. Damascus

20. God sent _____ a dream telling him to visit Saul on Straight Street in Damascus.
     a. Barnabas   b. Ananias   c. Luke

21. The letters Paul wrote to the churches were called _____ .
     a. notes   b. epistles   c. gospels

22. _____ wrote the book of Acts.
     a. Barnabas   b. Ananias   c. Luke

Answer true or false (each answer, 3 points).

23. _____ Saul's father was a Pharisee.

24. _____ Saul's parents sent him to Jerusalem for religious instruction.

25. _____ Saul traveled to Tarsus to persecute Christians.

26. _____ Saul was lifted over the city wall of Damascus in a basket.

27. _____ The Christians in Jerusalem were eager to accept Saul when he arrived
                  there after his conversion.

28. _____ Saul changed his name to Paul after becoming a Christian.

29. _____ Saul was imprisoned for spreading the good news of Christ.

30. _____ During his life, Saul went on one missionary journey.

Fill in the blanks with the missing books which were written by Paul (each answer, 2 points).

31. Romans   1 Thessalonians

     1 Corinthians   2 Thessalonians

     a. _____   1 Timothy

     Galatians   2 Timothy

     b. _____   d. _____

     Philippians   e. _____

     c. _____

     Date _____
     Score _____
     Possible Score _____ 100 _____

52

Name _____

Answer *true* or *false* (each answer, 2 points).
1. _____ It is best to sit at a desk to read the Bible.
2. _____ You should try to read the Bible at least five minutes a day.
3. _____ Principles in the Bible are timeless.
4. _____ We will be unhappy if we obey everything God tells us to do.
5. _____ Memorizing Scripture will help you not to be afraid.
6. _____ We should not share our food with the poor.
7. _____ God is proud of a lazy person.
8. _____ Parents should never discipline their children.

Write the correct word on each line. One word will be used twice (each answer, 2 points).

commands	heart	promises
copy	memorize	sin
everyone	principles	spiritual

9. We are told what to do by the _____ in the Bible.
10. Three things you should especially look for as you read the Bible are a._____, b._____, and c._____.
11. Memorizing Scripture will help you not to_____.
12. The Bible is written for_____.
13. The Bible says to trust in the Lord with all your_____.
14. What daily eating is to your physical life, daily Bible reading is to your _____ life.
15. In order to hide God's Word in your heart, you should_____ Scripture.
16. The steps in memorizing are _____ , read, say, tell, and restudy.

Write the correct letter and answer on each line (each answer, 3 points).
17. Wisdom comes from _____.
a. words b. God c. food
18. A wise saying is called a_____.
a. word b. joke c. proverb
19. The Book of Proverbs was written by_____.
a. David b. Paul c. Solomon
20. If we obey God's commands we will be_____.
a. happy b. sad c. fat
21. "Thy Word is a lamp unto my _____."
a. head b. heart c. feet
22. Hot tempers cause_____.
a. friendships b. patience c. arguments

23. A gossip can never keep a _____.
    a. quarrel   b. secret   c. argument
24. Memorizing Scripture will help you share your love for _____.
    a. God   b. dogs   c. yourself

Match these items (each answer, 2 points).

25. _____	physical	a. a wise saying
26. _____	daily	b. bodily
27. _____	timeless	c. every day
28. _____	proverb	d. command
29. _____	generous	e. giving much
		f. having no beginning nor ending

Write three proverbs you memorized (each answer, 5 points).
30. _____

    _____

    _____

31. _____

    _____

    _____

32. _____

    _____

    _____

Put the steps for memorizing Scripture in the correct order by writing
the letters in order on the lines (each answer, 3 points).

33. _____	a. Restudy it for several days.
34. _____	b. Tell it to someone else.
35. _____	c. Read each sentence aloud ten times.
36. _____	d. Say it aloud from memory.
37. _____	e. Copy the verse from the Bible.

Date _____
Score _____
Possible Score _____ **100** _____

Name _____

Match these items (each answer, 2 points).

1.	_____	the Lord is my shepherd	a.	in green pastures
2.	_____	He maketh me to lie down	b.	runneth over
3.	_____	He leadeth me	c.	with oil
4.	_____	He restoreth	d.	shall follow me
5.	_____	Thy rod and Thy staff	e.	through the valley
6.	_____	Thou anointest my head	f.	beside the still
7.	_____	my cup		waters
8.	_____	surely goodness and mercy	g.	they comfort me
9.	_____	I will dwell	h.	I shall not want
			i.	my soul
			j.	in the house of the
				Lord forever

Choose the best word to complete each sentence and write it on the line (each answer, 3 points).

David	Good Shepherd	King Ahab
God	Jesus	King Darius
Goliath	Jew	King Saul

10. The shepherd of the Twenty-Third Psalm is _____.
11. The writer of the Twenty-Third Psalm is _____.
12. Jesus said, "I am the _____."
13. Daniel was a_____.
14. David's music made_____ feel better.
15. Daniel was protected in the lions' den by_____.
16. God helped David kill_____.
17. Daniel was chosen to be a ruler by_____ because Daniel was faithful.

Write *true* or *false* (each answer, 2 points).

18.	_____	David wrote only one Psalm—the Twenty-Third Psalm.
19.	_____	The shepherd looks for a sheep when it gets lost.
20.	_____	Twenty men wanted to fight Goliath.
21.	_____	The shepherd in the Twenty-Third Psalm is David.
22.	_____	Daniel was born in Babylonia.
23.	_____	Daniel had more power than everyone but the king.
24.	_____	King Darius wanted Daniel to die.
25.	_____	Only one lion bit Daniel.
26.	_____	God protected Daniel from the lions.
27.	_____	God helped David kill the lion and bear.

Write the correct letter and answer on each line (each answer, 2 points).

28.   *Restore* means *to* _____ .
        a. *take away*   b. *put back*   c. *repeat*

29.   *Paths of righteousness* means_____ .
        a. *sheep paths*   b. *right paths*   c. *paths in heaven*

30.   *Mercy* means_____ .
        a. *gifts*   b. *charity*   c. *kindness we do not deserve*

31.   *Anoint* means to_____ .
        a. *rub with oil*   b. *kiss*   c. *appoint*

32.   The shepherd's job is to_____ .
        a. lead his sheep   b. drive his sheep   c. let his sheep wander

33.   The "House of the Lord" is_____ .
        a. Bethlehem   b. heaven   c. Jerusalem

34.   The shepherd's rod and staff are to _____ .
        a. beat sheep   b. comfort sheep   c. scare sheep

Complete each statement (each answer, 4 points).

35.   The Twenty-Third_____ tells us about God's care.

36.   David was the author of many of the_____ .

37.   Daniel was cast into the_____ .

38.   The giant Goliath was killed by _____ .

39.   The shepherd _____ his sheep.

40.   The Good Shepherd is _____ .

Date _____
Score
Possible Score _____ 100

56

Name _____

Answer *true* or *false* (each answer, 2 points).
1. _____ God is like the wind—you cannot see Him but you can see what He does.
2. _____ God likes to punish people.
3. _____ Jesus took our punishment for sin.
4. _____ God promised the Jews a Savior.
5. _____ All religions believe in the same god.

Write the correct letter and answer on each line (each answer, 3 points).
6. Psalm 100:3 "Know ye that the Lord He is God: it is He that hath _____us and not we ourselves...."
   a. taught   b. made   c. seen
7. Life is in the _____.
   a. brain   b. liver   c. blood
8. Romans 6:23 "...the gift of God is _____ through Jesus Christ our Lord."
   a. eternal life   b. babies   c. good health
9. The greatest wonder of all creation is _____.
   a. earth   b. our bodies   c. trees
10. All men have an inner need to _____.
   a. worship God   b. have a pet   c. drive a car

Write the correct word on the line (each answer, 4 points).
Bible	earth	God	made
children	exists	heaven	Savior

11. Bible writers were told what to write by _____.
12. God promised Abraham many _____.
13. Before He came to earth Jesus was in _____.
14. God speaks to us through the _____.
15. Thomas Aquinas wrote laws to prove God _____.

Match these items (each answer, 3 points).
16. _____ Sarah   a.   father of a nation
17. _____ Abraham   b.   Jesus' father
18. _____ God   c.   Sarai
19. _____ Canaan   d.   Savior
20. _____ Jesus   e.   Israel

Write the following verses from the Bible from memory (each answer, 5 points).

21.   Psalm 139:14 _____

_____

22.   Psalm 100:3 _____

_____

23.   John 1:12 _____

_____

24.   Romans 6:23 _____

_____

Answer these questions (each answer, 4 points).

25.   What did God promise Abram that He would make of him?

_____

_____

26.   Whom had God promised to the Jews hundreds of years ago?

_____

_____

27.   How do we know that God exists?

_____

_____

28.   Why should you read the Bible?

_____

_____

29.   What is man's most important need?

_____

_____

_____

Date _____
Score _____
Possible Score _____ 100 _____

Name _____

Complete these sentences with words from the list. Words may be used more than once (each answer, 3 points).

agriculture	Euphrates	new tools
customs	Jordan	spring
Dead Sea	new ideas	systems of law and
deserts	New Jersey	government
domestication of animals	new products	Tigris

1. Canaan is about the size of the state of _____ .
2. The word that means *ways of living* is _____ .
3. Three ideas that began in Bible lands are a. _____ ,
    b. _____ ,
    and c._____ .
4. Three things exchanged along the trade routes in Bible times were
    a. _____ , b. _____ , and
    c. _____ .
5. The Fertile Crescent included land along three rivers. They are the
    a. _____ , b._____ , and
    c. _____ .
6. The lowest point east of the Mediterranean Sea is the _____ .
7. The Holy Land has mountains, lakes, and _____ .
8. Another name for the Salt Sea is the _____ .
9. Latter rains fell in the _____ .

Write this Bible verse from memory (this answer, 5 points).
10. Genesis 12:2 _____
    _____
    _____
    _____
    _____
    _____

Match these items (each answer, 2 points).

11.	_____	the land watered by the Nile River	a.	Egypt
12.	_____	Abram's nephew	b.	Isaac
13.	_____	word used in Hebrew name to say	c.	Lot
		place has a well	d.	Sarah
14.	_____	God changed his name to Israel	e.	Beer
15.	_____	sold by his brothers into slavery in	f.	Jacob
		Egypt	g.	Joseph
16.	_____	kings of Egypt	h.	Pharaoh
17.	_____	Abraham's son	i.	famine
18.	_____	time when crops fail and people go	j.	Moses
		hungry	k.	Exodus
19.	_____	led God's people out of slavery in		
		Egypt		
20.	_____	Abraham's wife		

Complete the following sentences (each answer, 3 points).

21. Abram was called a nomad because he _____ .
22. The name of one river of the Fertile Crescent is the _____ .
23. After they left Egypt, the children of Israel wandered for forty years in the _____ .
24. The saltiness of the Dead Sea is caused by _____ .
25. The ways people live are _____ .
26. We call Canaan the "_____ Land."
27. The name *Israel* means _____ .
28. The Philistines filled the wells of Abraham with _____ .
29. The climate of the Holy Land is affected by the _____ of the land.
30. When land grows good crops it is called _____ .

Date _____
Score _____
Possible Score _____ **100** _____

Name _____

Match these items (each answer, 3 points).

1. _____ publican
2. _____ sin
3. _____ Pharisee
4. _____ sparrows
5. _____ hare
6. _____ Jesus
7. _____ eternal
8. _____ a mind
9. _____ a heart
10. _____ a will

a. asked God for wisdom
b. lost the race to the tortoise
c. causes death
d. God takes care of them
e. to understand
f. was sorry for his sins
g. boasted that he did not act like others
h. to love
i. Lord of Lords
j. died for our sins
k. no beginning nor end
l. to do

Write the correct letter and answer on each line (each answer, 3 points).

11. A parable is a _____ .
 a. story with a lesson
 b. fable
 c. poem

12. Aesop wrote _____ .
 a. poetry   b. fables   c. parables

13. Moses wrote_____ .
 a. fables
 b. Psalms
 c. the first five books of the Bible

14. Man was made _____ .
 a. in God's image
 b. for himself alone
 c. for the angels

15. The Father cares about everything in heaven _____ .
 a. and the skies
 b. and on earth
 c. but not sinners

16. To *adopt* means to _____ .
 a. *drop*
 b. *forget*
 c. *take as your own child*

17. God has _____ .
 a. no beginning nor end
 b. a beginning only
 c. an end only

18. God wants us to _____ .
    a. love only our brothers
    b. hate our brothers
    c. love Him and all people
19. King Solomon was _____ .
    a. David's son
    b. David's grandfather
    c. David's father
20. Jesus was without _____ .
    a. sin   b. tears   c. happiness

Write from memory the following Bible verses (each answer, 5 points).

21. Matthew 10:30 and 31 _____
    _____
    _____
    _____

22. Psalm 100:3 _____
    _____
    _____
    _____

23. Psalm 139:14 _____
    _____
    _____
    _____

24. Matthew 7:8 _____
    _____
    _____
    _____

Write *true* or *false* (each answer, 2 points).

25. _____ "King of Kings" and "Lord of Lords" are both titles of God.
26. _____ Solomon asked God for wisdom.
27. _____ God gave man a will to do what he wants to do.
28. _____ David killed Goliath with a bow and arrow.
29. _____ *Fearing* God means *knowing* and *respecting* God.
30. _____ God wants you to know that you are His child.
31. _____ I should love and obey God only because it makes me happy.
32. _____ God never sleeps.
33. _____ God adopts us when we are good.
34. _____ When you are afraid, you should trust in God.

Date _____

Score _____

Possible Score _____ 100 _____

Name _____

Answer *true* or *false* (each answer, 2 points).
1. _____ Jesus' disciples follow Him.
2. _____ A captive captures someone.
3. _____ Isaiah tells about Jesus.
4. _____ Psalms is a book of praise.
5. _____ We should strive to be first.
6. _____ Jesus' command is for all disciples.
7. _____ John persecuted the Christians.
8. _____ Jesus cried over Capernaum and its lost people.
9. _____ We must earn God's love.
10. _____ Be a hearer and a doer.

Match these items (each answer, 2 points).

11. _____	in prison in Rome	a.	Jesus and God
12. _____	guards	b.	water
13. _____	blood	c.	Satan
14. _____	in the beginning was	d.	stoned for witnessing
15. _____	sinners	e.	doing for others
16. _____	woman of Samaria	f.	disciples
17. _____	wants disobedience to God	g.	John
18. _____	Dorcas	h.	talk and actions
19. _____	Stephen	i.	acts of charity
20. _____	cousin to Jesus	j.	saints of Caesar's household
21. _____	mercy	k.	Paul
22. _____	showing love to Jesus	l.	covers sins
		m.	kindness and pity
		n.	all people

Write three correct letters and answers on the lines (each answer, 1 point).

23. You witness by a. _____ , b. _____ ,
    and c. _____ .
    a. kind acts   c. going to the right people
    b. telling of Jesus   d. guarding your tongue

24. You love Jesus by a. _____ ,
    b. _____ , and c. _____ .
    a. keeping His commandments   c. witnessing
    b. loving others   d. being happy

25. Jesus calls us a. _____ , b. _____ ,
    and c. _____ .
    a. friends   c. apostles
    b. disciples   d. doers

26. When you are mistreated, you a. _____ , b. _____ ,
    and c. _____ .
    a. do good to that person   c. pray for the person
    b. tell others about it   d. turn the other cheek

27. Three people who said Jesus is the Son of God were a. _____ ,
    b. _____ , and c. _____ .
    a. the thieves on the crosses   c. the centurion
    b. Paul   d. John

Write the correct letter and answer on the line (each answer, 2 points).

28. Of the people listed, the Old Testament prophet is _____ .
    a. Mordecai   c. Malachi
    b. Manasses   d. Matthew

29. Of the people listed, the disciple of Jesus is _____ .
    a. Moses   c. Micah
    b. Matthew   d. Margaret

30. "From the same mouth come blessing and cursing," is found in
    _____ .
    a. John 3:10   c. James 3:10
    b. Jude 3:10   d. Luke 3:10

31. "Thou shalt have no other gods before me," is found in
    _____ .
    a. Genesis 20:3   c. Exodus 1:3
    b. Exodus 20:3

32. The main thought of John 3:16 is _____
    _____ .
    a. some people will perish
    b. the ones who believe in Jesus are saved
    c. some people will not believe in Jesus

33. I believe the Bible because _____ .
    a. I want to   c. it is the word of prophets
    b. my teacher tells me to   d. it is God's Word

34. A prophet tells _____ .
    a. what could happen   c. God's message
    b. what God says might happen d. what he thinks is God's
                                      message

Complete these statements (each answer, 3 points).
35. Jesus said that if we love Him we will keep His _____ .
36. If Jesus had not risen from the dead, He could not _____ us.
37. Paul wrote letters to both people and _____ .
38. Paul witnessed everywhere, even in _____ .
39. James said in his Epistle that a part of our body that often causes
    trouble is the _____ .
40. Old Testament prophets told many things about _____ .
41. John said that we are lying if we say we love God but hate our

    _____ .
42. When you tell someone what God has done for you, you are a _____ .
43. The name *Jesus* means _____ .

Date _____
Score _____
Possible Score _____ **100** _____

Name _____

Answer *true* or *false* (each answer, 2 points).

1. _____ My worth comes from God.
2. _____ Believe in yourself and you can do anything.
3. _____ Jesus and good works get us to heaven.
4. _____ Daniel was thrown into a den of lions because he worshiped a false god.
5. _____ Peter's brother brought him to Jesus.
6. _____ Memorizing Scripture will help you not to sin.
7. _____ We will be happy if we obey what God tells us in the Bible.
8. _____ Commands tell us what to do.
9. _____ The Fertile Crescent is where the farmers lived in Canaan.
10. _____ Canaan was about the size of New Jersey.
11. _____ Geography tells a lot about how people must live.
12. _____ A place where something happens is called its setting.

Write the correct letter and answer on each line (each answer, 3 points).

13. The writer of the Twenty-Third Psalm is _____ .
   a. Paul   b. David   c. Solomon
14. You can learn God's knowledge by _____ .
   a. reading your Bible
   b. going to college
   c. watching television
15. The book that tells the story of creation is _____ .
   a. Acts   b. Genesis   c. Proverbs
16. Wisdom comes from _____ .
   a. food   b. words   c. God
17. If we obey God's principles we will be _____ .
   a. sad   b. happy   c. fat
18. The book of Proverbs was written by _____ .
   a. Solomon   b. David   c. Paul
19. The greatest wonder of all God's creation is the _____ .
   a. earth   b. ocean   c. body
20. Today we call Canaan _____ .
   a. the Holy Land   b. Egypt   c. the United States

Match these items (each answer, 2 points).

21. _____ adopted   a. a wise saying
22. _____ gospel   b. followers
23. _____ witness   c. land of promise
24. _____ disciples   d. good news
25. _____ proverb   e. wrote laws to prove God exists
26. _____ Aquinas
                            f. to take for one's own
                            g. tell what you know

Write the correct word on each line. Choose from these words (each answer, 3 points).

Bible	knowledge
commands	physical
Epistles	restudy
God	spiritual
Jesus	timeless

27.   The letters Paul wrote the churches were called _____ .

28.   The Good Shepherd is _____ .

29.   The steps to memorizing Scripture are copy, read, say, tell, and

_____ .

30.   God tells us what to do or what not to do by

_____ in the Bible.

31.   God told us to seek this above all things: _____ .

32.   The Bible writers were told what to write by _____ .

33.   Daily Bible reading will make you strong in your _____ life.

34.   In order not to sin, you need a _____ of God's Word.

Complete these verses (each answer, 4 points).

35.   "Surely goodness and mercy _____

_____

_____ ." Psalm 23:6

36.   "For God so loved the world, that He gave his only begotten Son,

_____ ."

_____ John 3:16

37.   "...Go ye into all the world, and _____

_____ ." Mark 16:15

38.   "Know ye that the Lord he is God: it is He that hath made us, and
       not we ourselves; _____

_____

_____ ." Psalm 100:3

Date _____

Score _____

Possible Score _____ **100** _____

Notes

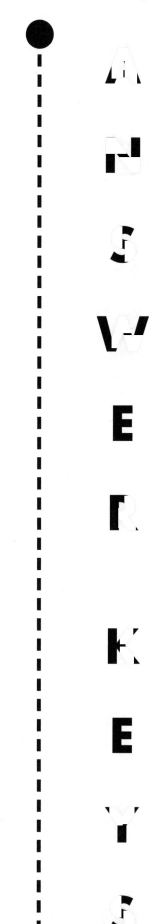

LIFEPAC

ANSWER KEYS

SECTION ONE

1.1 a. L a m b o f G o d
b. t w o
c. f o l l o w e d J e s u s
d. A n d r e w
e. S i m o n P e t e r
f. b r o u g h t P e t e r t o
J e s u s
g. g a v e S i m o n a new n a m e
h. a s t o n e
i. t a k e a w a y s i n
j. J e s u s t a k e s a w a y s i n.

1.2 Map activity
teacher check

1.3 a. Interviews will vary.
b.

1.4 a. Interviews will vary.
b.

1.5 Letters will vary.

1.6 teacher check

1.7 Answers will vary.

1.8 Answers will vary

1.9 a. Matthew   g. Peter
b. James   h. Andrew
c. John   i. Bartholomew
d. Philip   j. James
e. Thomas   k. Thaddaeus
f. Judas   l. Simon

1.10 "A n d f o r g i v e u s o u r
d e b t s a s w e f o r g i v e
o u r d e b t o r s"
M a t t h e w   6:12

1.11 d

1.12 b

1.13 a

1.14 c

1.15 Verse: Acts 2:21
See 1.16 for wording.

1.16 "Whosoever shall call on the
name of the Lord shall be
saved."

1.17 Accounts will vary.

1.18 Across
1. Lamb
4. Bethsaida
6. men
Down
2. Andrew
3. forgiveness
5. sin

1.19 a. foun   tain
b. quar   ter
c. win   dow
d. Lin   da
e. for   give
f. af   ter
g. san   dal
h. fol   low

1.20 a. wor   ship
b. touch   ing
c. truth   ful
d. mean   while
e. breath   less
f. al   though
g. no   where

SECTION TWO

2.1 Verse: John 1:12
See 2.2 for wording

2.2 "But as many as received him, to them gave he power to become the sons of God, even to them that believe on his name:" John 1:12.

2.3 Down
1. forgives
4. died
5. Moses

Across
2. confess
3. Nicodemus

2.4
1. forgives — What God does with sin
2. confess — What we should do with sin
3. Nicodemus — Asked about the new birth
4. died — What Jesus did on the Cross for our sins
5. Moses — Made a bronze serpent

2.5 teacher check

2.6 Any order:
a. love
b. joy
c. peace
d. long-suffering
e. gentleness
f. goodness
g. faith
h. meekness
i. temperance

2.7 Galatians 5:22-23

2.8
a. came — coming
b. completed — completing
c. decided — deciding
d. excited — exciting
e. gave — giving
f. introduced — introducing
g. invited — inviting
h. lived — living
i. named — naming
j. received — receiving

2.9 Lists will vary.

SECTION ONE

1.1 Examples:
trees
lakes
mountains
animals

1.2 a. God created day and night.
b. God made the firmament.
c. God gathered the waters together to make dry land. God made plant life.
d. God made the sun, moon and stars.
e. God made the birds and animals and blessed them.
f. God created man in His own image.
g. God rested from His work.

1.3 Example:
God knows all. God knows what is best. God could create the world. God knows us best.

1.4 a million years and a day

1.5 when the stars have passed away

1.6 Hint:
He will still be living and loving.

1.7 a. all
b. heaven
c. earth
d. thrones
e. him
f. for

1.8 teacher check

1.9 Revelation 4:11 – "Thou art worthy, O Lord, to receive glory and honour and power: for thou hast created all things, and for thy pleasure they are and were created."

1.10 Any order:
a. He made me.
b. He cares for me.
c. He helps me with His knowledge.

1.11 b
1.12 d
1.13 a
1.14 e
1.15 c
1.16 d
1.17 b
1.18 f
1.19 e
1.20 a
1.21 c
1.22 a. 3 2 2
b. 3 2 2
c. 2 2 2
d. 2 1 1
e. 2 2 2
1.23 I Peter 5:7
1.24 Proverbs 2:6
1.25 Genesis 2:22
1.26 Psalms 100:3
1.27 Colossians 2:3
1.28 Genesis 1:1
1.29 Matthew 6:33

SECTION TWO

2.1   Example:
Reading the Bible will help you have a stronger faith. You will understand more of what God is saying to you. You will learn more of His knowledge.

2.2   true

2.3   false

2.4   true

2.5   true

2.6   false

2.7   true

2.8   false

2.9   Examples:
    a. The Bible and signs of Jesus written in it were written to help people believe in Jesus that they may have eternal life.
    b. Jesus was to be the Savior of the world.
    c. God's holy men wrote the Bible. The Holy Ghost, or Spirit, inspired them.
    d. Scripture is given by God and used for doctrine, reproof, correction, and instruction in righteousness.
    e. Reading God's Word and thinking about it helps us keep from doing wrong.

2.10   a. "Jesus saith unto him, Have I been so long time with you, and yet hast thou not known me, Philip? he that hath seen me hath seen the Father; and how sayest thou then, Shew us the Father?"
    b. Jesus saith unto him, I am the way, the truth, and the life: no man cometh unto the Father, but by me."

2.11   Jesus

2.12   Examples:
    a. Prays for you
    b. Gives you heavenly thoughts and desires
    c. Helps you understand the Bible

2.13   When you accept Jesus as your Savior

2.14   c

2.15   e

2.16   g

2.17   a

2.18   b

2.19   f

2.20   d

2.21   weakness

2.22   to help someone by speaking for them

2.23   sounds made from pain or sorrow

2.24   spoken

2.25   Example:
We know not what to pray, but the Holy Spirit helps our weaknesses by speaking for us with sounds of pain or sorrow which cannot be spoken.

2.26   Examples:
    a. I am thankful for my family. I am thankful for my school.
    b. I love God for giving me salvation. I love God for watching over me.
    c. I forgot to pray today. I got angry at my best friend.
    d. My mother
        My father
    e. I need to be kinder to my brother. I need to study the Bible more.

2.27   Example:
        I may pray to God as often as I wish.
        He always welcomes my prayers.
2.28   to love one another

2.29   Examples:
        a. by accepting Jesus
        b. by praying
        c. by reading the Bible
        d. by witnessing to others

2.30   Example:
        I will be doing as God's Word has
        told me. God said in His Word that
        I should obey my parents.

2.31   Example:
        By obeying His Word, we show our love
        for Him. (John 15:10)
2.32   a. Salvation   d. Faith
        b. Righteousness   e. Gospel of Peace
        c. Truth   f. Spirit
2.33   a. bee   hive
        b. cotton   wood
        c. flash   light
        d. frame   work
        e. gentle   men
        f. head   quarters
        g. light   house
        h. news   paper
        i. wind   shield

SECTION THREE

3.1   Example:
        I will live a more Christ-like
        life. I will pray, read the Bible,
        and tell others of Jesus.

3.2   true

3.3   true

3.4   false

3.5   true

3.6   false

3.7   a. world
        b. Son
        c. life
3.8   a. we
        b. Christ
        c. died
3.9   a. whole
        b. world
3.10   a. new
        b. creature

3.11   a. all
        b. sinned
3.12   a. power
        b. sons
        c. of
        d. God
        e. believe
3.13   a. (e stēm') to place a high value upon
        b. (u flikt') to hurt and cause pain
        c. (trans gresh' un) the breaking
            of a law or rule
        d. (i nik' wi tē) a very bad act
        e. (chas tīz' ment) punishment
        f. (u strā') to go apart from the
            right way
3.14   teacher check
3.15   Any order:
        a. Walk worthy of the Lord.
        b. Be fruitful in good works.
        c. Increase in the knowledge
            of God.
3.16   teacher check
3.17   Example:
        Because He loves us and
        knows what is best for us.

SECTION FOUR

4.1 Example:
Do not keep little
children from coming to Christ.

4.2 Example:
You will find God if
you seek Him.

4.3 Example: God loves those that
love Him and those that try to
find Him shall find Him.

4.4 a. Foretelling the future
b. A person who casts spells
c. Supposed to have supernatural powers
d. Person who talks with the dead
e. Something that God hates

4.5 All people who do these things are
an abomination to the Lord.

4.6 From God

4.7 The fear of the Lord

4.8 Happy

4.9 Ways of pleasantness

4.10 d

4.11 a

4.12 e

4.13 b

4.14 c

4.15 Example:
People who are wise still
seek Jesus as Savior.

4.16 Example:
God knows best.

4.17 true

4.18 true

4.19 false

4.20 true

SECTION ONE

1.1	false		1.16	a
1.2	false		1.17	c
1.3	true		1.18	true
1.4	true		1.19	false
1.5	true		1.20	false
1.6	false		1.21	true
1.7	true		1.22	c
1.8	true		1.23	b
1.9	c		1.24	e
1.10	d		1.25	a
1.11	e		1.26	d
1.12	b		1.27	true
1.13	a		1.28	true
1.14	b		1.29	false
1.15	c		1.30	false

SECTION TWO

2.1	1		2.16	humble confuse
2.2	5		2.17	keep
2.3	3		2.18	remember come
2.4	4		2.19	realize fulfill
2.5	2		2.20	sudden promise
2.6	true		2.21	rise
2.7	false		2.22	appear
2.8	true		2.23	eager wonder
2.9	false			
2.10	false			
2.11	b			
2.12	a			
2.13	b			
2.14	c			
2.15	a			

SECTION THREE

3.1   Mister

3.2   Street

3.3   pound

3.4   Reverend

3.5   Doctor

3.6   Saint

3.7   yard

3.8   Across: Down:
1. Pharisees   1. Persecuted
3. Jerusalem   2. Saul
5. Acts   4. Luke
6. Jesus   7. Synagogue
8. Stephen
9. Rabbi
10. Damascus

3.9   Romans
1 Corinthians
2 Corinthians
Galatians
Ephesians
Philippians
Colossians
1 Thessalonians
2 Thessalonians
1 Timothy
2 Timothy
Titus
Philemon

3.10 epistles

3.11 sinners, worst

3.12 God

3.13 churches

3.14 robbed

3.15 three

3.16 a. mon/ey
b. com/et
c. eat/en
d. cred/it
e. cab/in
f. pal/ace

3.17 a. pre/pare
b. e/nough
c. glo/bal
d. cra/zy
e. re/form
f. Je/sus

3.18 a. be/have   open
b. gra/vy   open
c. tra/vel   closed
d. fi/nal   open
e. bro/ken   open
f. ba/by   open
g. pon/der   closed
h. hon/ey   closed
i. e/ven   open
j. ho/ly   open

3.19 false

3.20 true

3.21 true

3.22 false

3.23 true

SECTION ONE

1.1   a. spiritual
      b. physical
1.2   five
1.3   Dwight L. Moody
1.4   false
1.5   false
1.6   true
1.7   false
1.8   true
1.9   teacher check
1.10 a. come unto me
      b. I will give you rest
1.11 a. believe on Jesus
      b. you will be saved
1.12 a. honour thy father and mother
      b. It will be well with you.
         You will live long on the earth.
1.13 teacher check
1.14 Give instruction to a wise man,
      and he will be yet wiser.
1.15 Any order:
      a. commands
      b. promises
      c. principles
1.16 true
1.17 true
1.18 false
1.19 false

1.20 true
1.21 false
1.22 commands
1.23 principles
1.24 promises
1.25 children
1.26 prayer
1.27 pencil or pen
1.28 keep alert
1.29 find a message
1.30 in the Bible
1.31 feet
1.32 path
1.33 everyone
1.34 sit up
1.35 hab' it
1.36 ex pect'
1.37 dis turb'
1.38 be cause'
1.39 note' book
1.40 re mem' ber
1.41 un der stand'
1.42 im por' tant
1.43 or' di nar y

SECTION TWO

2.1   b
2.2   d

2.3   a
2.4   c

2.5	a	2.12	Bible
2.6	c	2.13	ten
2.7	Thy word is a lamp unto my feet and a light unto my path.	2.14	mind
		2.15	memory
2.8	a. sin	2.16	Tell
	b. afraid	2.17	Restudy
	c. love	2.18	animal
	d. Jesus	2.19	carry
2.9	yes	2.20	make
2.10	yes		
2.11	a. o		
	b. ea		
	c. a		
	d. e		
	e. eu		

SECTION THREE

3.1	Jim's parents didn't like the way Brad behaved.	3.15	teacher check
		3.16	Example: Betty helped Sue.
3.2	Jim went anyway. Jim disobeyed his father.	3.17	yes
3.3	Jim's dad spanked him.	3.18	They shared what they had with someone who had nothing.
3.4	Jim asked God to forgive him.	3.19	a. walks with wise men.
3.5	yes		b. is a companion (friend) of fools, shall be destroyed
3.6	Solomon		
3.7	a. wise sayings	3.20	a. makes his father glad
3.8	a. wise		b. despises his mother
3.9	teacher check	3.21	a. heareth his father's instruction
3.10	b. obeying God		b. heareth not rebuke
3.11	Patty got into trouble because she didn't obey.	3.22	a. fears God
			b. despises wisdom and instruction
3.12	Any order:	3.23	teacher check
	a. She ran across the street.	3.24	He wants me to work hard to get the job done.
	b. She ran in front of a truck.		
	c. She got a spanking.	3.25	teacher check
3.13	yes	3.26	b. wisdom and understanding
3.14	teacher check		

3.27 a. shining brightly
3.28 a. think they are right
3.29 b. go away from foolish people
3.30 a. have hot violent tempers
3.31 a. quiets anger
3.32 teacher check
3.33 talebearer
3.34 Lying lips
3.35 froward mouth, perverse lips
3.36 talebearer
3.37 true

3.38 false
3.39 true
3.40 b, d, e, f, g
3.41 teacher check
3.42 teacher check
3.43 teacher check
3.44 teacher check
3.45 teacher check
3.46 teacher check
3.47 teacher check
3.48 teacher check

SECTION ONE

1.1	teacher check	1.20	fields
1.2	The Lord is my shepherd; I shall not want.	1.21	follower
		1.22	quiet
1.3	Lord Jesus	1.23	put back
1.4	my	1.24	sinless
1.5	need	1.25	true
1.6	Good Shepherd	1.26	true
1.7	teacher check	1.27	false
1.8	Either order:	1.28	true
	a. grass	1.29	false
	b. water	1.30	teacher check
1.9	God's Word (Bible)	1.31	thorns
1.10	Either order:	1.32	anoints
	a. grass	1.33	water
	b. water	1.34	staff
	God's Word (Bible)	1.35	rod
1.11	The water gets into the sheep's wool. If the wool gets wet and heavy, the sheep may fall into the water and float down the stream.	1.36	Thou preparest a table before me in the presence of mine enemies: thou anointest my head with oil; my cup runneth over.
1.12	yes	1.37	b. David
1.13	yes	1.38	a. kindness when we do not deserve it
1.14	d. a, b, and c	1.39	b. heaven
1.15	b. right paths	1.40	no
1.16	b. shepherd	1.41	teacher check
1.17	b. Lord Jesus	1.42	A person who has accepted Jesus as his or her Savior will be ready for heaven.
1.18	a. leads the sheep		
1.19	He restoreth my soul: he leadeth me in the paths of righteousness for his name's sake.		

1.43
   a. want
   b. pastures
   c. waters
   d. soul
   e. righteousness
   f. death
   g. staff
   h. table
   i. oil
   j. cup
   k. goodness
   l. mercy
   m. house

1.44   Example:
The Lord is my helper; I shall not worry. He helps me to sleep at night.

SECTION TWO

2.1	David	2.18	4
2.2	a round	2.19	robbers
2.3	a bout		bears
2.4	pa rade		lions
2.5	chick en		danger
2.6	true		snakes
2.7	false		trouble
2.8	false	2.20	God
2.9	true	2.21	He had disobeyed God.
2.10	Example: If a wild animal were to try to climb over the fold, the thorns would keep it out.	2.22	yes
		2.23	yes
		2.24	King
2.11	Example: David would go and look for the sheep. David would call the sheep by its name.	2.25	Bring
		2.26	string
		2.27	sing
2.12	Example: The sheep could drown.	2.28	praises
		2.29	Goliath
2.13	2	2.30	David's father
2.14	3	2.31	David
2.15	5	2.32	Saul
2.16	6	2.33	David
2.17	1	2.34	2
			3
			1

2.35	3
	2
	1
2.36	3
	5
	1
	4
	2

2.37   God

2.38   Example:
        David had been a shepherd.

SECTION THREE

3.1   excellent

3.2   a.   faithful
      b.   fault

3.3   Jerusalem

3.4   He and his people had been captured by Babylonian soldiers.

3.5   Everything Daniel did pleased the king.

3.6   trick

3.7   den

3.8   stone

3.9   pray

3.10   law

3.11   He decided to obey God and honor Him first of all.

3.12   b.   God helped him

3.13   a.   God protected him

3.14   b.   God helped him

3.15   cage

3.16   position

3.17   match

3.18   page

3.19   courage

3.20   ditch

3.21   Daniel was hurried to the lion's den.

3.22   The angel touched the lions and they closed their mouths.

3.23   The next morning the king rushed to the den.

3.24   Daniel was not harmed.

3.25   The wicked princes were cast into the den.

3.26   Daniel lived many more years.

3.27   Living God

SECTION ONE

1.1	4
	1
	3
	2
1.2	2
	1
	3
	4
1.3	Abram; Abraham
1.4	Sarai; Sarah
1.5	children
1.6	Savior
1.7	hurt
1.8	a. God
	b. people
1.9	Canaan
1.10	teacher check
1.11	God
1.12	heaven
1.13	die
1.14	sin
1.15	Canaan

1.16	Abraham
1.17	aloud, allowed
1.18	bare, bear
1.19	whole, hole
1.20	sail, sale
1.21	Do, dew
1.22	a
1.23	ence
1.24	i
1.25	lop
1.26	qual
1.27	easily
1.28	alone
1.29	equal
1.30	science
1.31	gallop

SECTION TWO

2.1	true
2.2	true
2.3	false
2.4	true
2.5	false
2.6	false
2.7	true

2.8	false
2.9	a. complain
2.10	b. adventure
2.11	a. content (happy)
2.12	b. important
2.13	powerful, maker, perfect, needed

2.14 false

2.15 false

2.16 true

2.17 true

2.18 a. Some think the world began with an explosion that set the stars and planets in motion.

b. Some think the sun threw off pieces which became stars and planets.

2.19 Bible

2.20 200 billion

2.21

2.22 round
2.23 sea
2.24 snowfall
2.25 kind
2.26 flood
2.27 God told them what to write. God knows everything.
2.28 Example:
Eyes can see color, shape, size, and distance.

2.29 Example:
Each bone is made for a special purpose. Bones grow.
2.30 Example:
Skin stretches as you grow.
2.31 Example:
There are more than 600 muscles in my body.

2.32 Example:
The heart pushes seven tons of blood every day.

2.33 Example:
Lungs work without my thinking.

2.34 Example:
The nose warms the air for the lungs.

2.35 Example:
The outer ear is like a shell to catch sound. The inside of the ear is like a grand piano.
2.36 Example:
The blood is pushed by the heart pump. The blood never stops.

2.37 teacher check
2.38 teacher check
2.39 e
2.40 a
2.41 b
2.42 d

SECTION THREE

3.1 When people do not know the true God, they pray to gods made of wood or stone. They trust charms, rabbits' feet, or medals. They believe in more than one god. They may believe in wicked spirits.

3.2 yes

3.3 yes

3.4 yes

3.5 no

3.6 teacher check

3.7 "In the beginning God created the heaven and the earth." –fact, blue

3.8 Once there was a tiny thing that grew until it became the earth. –fiction, green (or) opinion, red

3.9 I think the universe just happened. –opinion, red

3.10 I believe Jesus was a good man but not a Savior. –opinion, red

3.11 Once upon a time there was a little chick, named Chicken Little. –fiction, green

3.12 Jesus said, "I am the way, the truth, and the life." –fact, blue

3.13 teacher check

3.14 Example:
The Bible tells the most about God, but we also learn of Him by observing the world around us.

3.15 God speaks to me through His word, the Bible.

3.16 Example:
God wants me to know His plan for my life.

3.17 God used forty men to write the Bible.

3.18 Examples:
a. The Bible tells that the earth is round.
b. The Bible tells of the value of snowfall and the part that lightning plays in the rainfall.
c. The Bible tells in the book of Genesis that animals will only bear their own kind.
or The Bible tells of the great Flood on earth.

3.19 teacher check

3.20 teacher check

3.21 Son

3.22 died

3.23 sin

3.24 God

3.25 false

3.26 false

3.27 true

3.28 true

3.29 true

3.30 true

3.31 true

3.32 he is God: it is he that hath made us and not we ourselves; we are his people, and the sheep of his pasture

3.33 am fearfully and wonderfully made: marvellous are thy works; and that my soul knoweth right well

3.34 eternal life through Jesus Christ our Lord

3.35 sons of God, even to them that believe on his name.

SECTION ONE

1.1 Example:
Geography is the study of everything
that is known about the earth
and the things and people
that live in it.

1.2 to get a better understanding of
Bible-land customs
to learn the setting of the events
recorded in the Bible

1.3 customs

1.4 southwestern Asia and northeastern
Africa (Egypt)

1.5 teacher check

1.6 Example:
It was in the center of civilization
and most of the events of the
Bible took place there.

1.7 Any order:
a. agriculture
b. domestication of animals
c. systems of law and government

1.8 Canaan

1.9 150 miles by 100 miles or a little
larger than New Jersey

1.10 Example:
The trade routes and army
routes usually went through these
lands.

1.11 Any order:
a. traders
b. armies
c. people from
neighboring countries

1.12 people from neighboring
countries

1.13 teacher check

1.14 a. Tigris
b. Jordan
c. Euphrates

1.15 false

1.16 false

1.17 true

1.18 true

1.19 Any order:
a. the crossroads of the ancient
world
b. the Fertile Crescent
c. the surface of the land

1.20 Mediterranean

1.21 Bethlehem

1.22 below

1.23 Dead Sea

1.24 Jerusalem

1.25 Example:
a. The boy's smile was an expression
of his happiness.
b. The hem on my mother's dress had
come loose.
c. Sharpening the pencil was just
a device to get out of his seat
and walk around the room.
d. The design on the front of the
book shows that it is a science
book.
e. My mother wanted to have both
profile and full-face pictures
of all the children.

1.26 10,082 feet

1.27 2,500 feet

1.28 a. coast
b. –al
c. agriculture
d. –al
e. tropic
f. –al
g. possess
h. –ion
i. express
j. –ion
k. invent
l. –ion

1.29 a. a wilderness, a dry land, and
         a desert
      b. seed time and harvest, cold and
         heat, and summer and winter,
         and day and night
      c. well-watered plain of Jordan
      d. mountains, hills, rivers,
         valleys
      e. upon some mountains or into
         some valley
      f. fire and hail; snow and vapors;
         stormy wind
      g. heat in a dry place
1.30 im por tant

1.31 ex pla na tion

1.32 Mes o po ta mi a

1.33 ex per i ence

1.34 par a graph

1.35 dif fer ence

1.36 de sign

1.37 teacher check

SECTION TWO

2.1   Euphrates

2.2   Padan-Aram

2.3   Sarai

2.4   brother's son or nephew

2.5   a. food
      b. water
2.6   a. God spoke to Abram.
      b. Abram and Lot left Haran.
      c. Abram got fruit at Damascus.
      d. Abram built an altar at
         Shechem.
      e. Abram came to Bethel.

2.7   An altar is a table, stand, or
      similar structure at which people
      worship or sacrifice.
2.8   He traveled around the country to find
      good places for the animals to feed.
2.9   Many nomads robbed people.
2.10 He built the altar to worship
      God, the Lord.
2.11 "And I will make of thee a great
      nation, and I will bless thee, and
      make thy name great; and thou
      shalt be a blessing."
2.12 spring
2.13 fall
2.14 plant the seed
2.15 swell the seed for harvesting

2.16 Example:
      In the highlands of Bethel were
      shrubs and grasses for the animals
      and food for people until the
      famine came. In the wilderness
      there was no food. In Egypt the
      Nile River made date and fruit trees
      and grain to grow.

2.17 teacher check
2.18 Sheep eat grass and are brown, black
      and white. Their meat is used for
      food, their wool to make clothing.
      Goats eat shrubs, bushes, thorny plants
      and are black. Their meat is used
      for food, their milk to drink and to
      make cheese and yogurt. Goat skins
      are used to make water bags. Goat
      hair is used for tent making.
2.19 They were jealous of Abraham's
      wealth and afraid of Isaac's
      large tribe.
2.20 well of seven
2.21 There is a well there.
2.22 Because he had had trouble with
      the Philistines.
2.23 desert
2.24 Sarah, Abraham's wife would have a son.
2.25 a. a. lion   b. bear
      b. wolf
      c. fox
      d. boar
      e. a. leopard   b. wolf

89

2.26 Across
1. flocks
4. Joseph
6. Hebron
Down
2. Shechem
3. Abraham
4. Jacob
5. herds

2.27 Famine
dry soil
dusty
hunger
no rain
Growing Food
harvesting
plowing
sowing
weeding

2.28 The land of Goshen was in the fertile part of Egypt.

2.29 a. cattle
b. corn

2.30 a. slaves
b. Pharaohs

2.31 Any order:
a. buildings
b. paintings
c. statues

2.32 south

2.33 a. land of the Philistines
b. tribes

2.34 a. paper
b. papyrus

2.35 a going out

2.36 teacher check

2.37 a. Succoth
b. Sea of Reeds
c. Rephidim
d. Mount Sinai
e. Kadesh-barnea
f. Mount Nebo

2.38 a piece of land almost surrounded by water

2.39 to put up a tent

2.40 forty years

2.41 on Mount Nebo

2.42 a. Asher
b. Benjamin
c. Dan
d. Ephraim
e. Gad
f. Issachar
g. Judah
h. Manasseh
i. Naphtali
j. Reuben
k. Simeon
l. Zebulun

2.43 teacher check

SECTION ONE

1.1 A proud heart is sin. We can not love people as God does if we think we are better than they are.

1.2 teacher check

1.3 Yes, because he helped them. Although he was an important man, George Washington was not proud. He was not too proud to do soldier's work.

1.4 Because Jesus was perfect. He loved everyone. He always thought of other people before He thought about Himself.

1.5 No, being important does not make one person better than another person.

1.6 Pharisee

1.7 Pharisee

1.8 false

1.9 false

1.10 true

1.11 false

1.12 teacher check

1.13 <u>Across</u>
1. temple
5. parable
6. rabbit
7. tithe
11. Aesop
12. law
13. love
<u>Down</u>
1. turtle
2. Pharisee
3. boast
4. fast
8. herbs
9. moral
10. fable

1.14 teacher check

1.15 importance

1.16 a. worthy
b. worthless
c. unworthy

1.17 teacher check

1.18 b. non-commissioned military officer who is higher in rank than a private
c. of the body

1.19 a. go without food
c. to move quickly

1.20 b. place of worship
c. the flat part on either side of your forehead

1.21 b. good in behavior
c. lesson or teaching

1.22 b. legal profession
c. a rule that must not be broken

1.23 teacher check

1.24 teacher check

1.25 d

1.26 a

1.27 b

1.28 f

1.29 e

1.30 SIN

1.31 sin

1.32 Son

1.33 Son

1.34 Son

1.35 The Son of God–Jesus

1.36 Jesus has taken the place of sin in my heart.

SECTION TWO

2.1 false

2.2 true

2.3 true

2.4 true

2.5 false

2.6 teacher check

2.7 God has made us in a wonderful way. Our bodies, minds, and so forth were made in a way to bring glory to God.

2.8 a. will
    b. heart
    c. mind

2.9 heart

2.10 mind

2.11 will

2.12 God made man like Himself. Man was made like God.

2.13 Yes. You love Him more when you learn more about His love or what God has done.

2.14 Study more of God's Word. Ask for wisdom and a heart to love.

2.15 teacher check

2.16 teacher check

2.17 teacher check

2.18 teacher check

2.19 God means He will never leave me. God will not leave me without help.

2.20 false

2.21 true

2.22 false

2.23 true

2.24 true

2.25 false

2.26 It might cause me to come to God. I could ask for God's help.

2.27 angels

2.28 Example
    Yes, I feel safe. God has given His angels charge over me

2.29 teacher check

2.30 a. earth
    b. everything
    c. God

2.31 a. belongs
    b. them

2.32 good

2.33 a. wealth
    b. His hands

2.34 a. pub li can
    b. Phar i see
    c. re li gious
    d. worth less ness
    e. Wash ing ton
    f. Tes ta ment
    g. char ac ter
    h. eve ry thing

2.35 a. Creator
    b. Father
    c. King
    d. Lord

2.36

2.37 Either order:
    a. heaven
    b. earth

2.38 Either order:
    a. Kings
    b. Lords

2.39 greater, or more

2.40 Any order:
    a. Creator
    b. Lord
    c. King
    d. Father

2.41 It means God is ruler over all the kings and lords of earth.

2.42 The children of God, everyone whom Jesus has saved.

2.43 teacher check

2.44

2.45 adopt
2.46 adopt
2.47 love
2.48 loves
2.49 die
2.50 family
2.51 His Son
2.52 laws
2.53 die

SECTION THREE

3.1 a. G
b. o
c. d
d. c
e. r
f. e
g. a
h. t
i. e
j. d
k. m
l. e
m. God created me.

3.2 God created all things for His glory.

3.3 I can glorify God by loving Him and obeying Him.

3.4 Fearing God means knowing and respecting God.

3.5 false

3.6 false

3.7 false
3.8 true
3.9 false
3.10 true
3.11 true

3.12 God loves me even when I am bad because God made me. I am God's child.

3.13 teacher check
3.14 teacher check
3.15 teacher check
3.16 teacher check

3.17 Example:
David ran to meet Goliath because David knew that God would protect him. David's weapon was a stone. He threw the stone and it hit Goliath in the forehead and he fell to the ground. David did not even have to use a sword to kill Goliath.

SECTION ONE

1.1 We show love to God by obeying Him.

1.2 He did not kill (destroy) all the animals of Amalek.

1.3 The Gospel (good news) of how He has lived and died for the sins of His people.

1.4 e

1.5 a

1.6 c

1.7 d

1.8 b

1.9 f

1.10 "If ye love me, keep my commandments." (John 14:15)

1.11 teacher check

1.12 teacher check

1.13 - 1.16 Examples:

1.13 Sin is still in our hearts and lives.

1.14 by letting God have control of our life, by the power of the Holy Spirit – (not by trying harder)

1.15 the Holy Spirit

1.16 He changed from being an enemy of Jesus to being a disciple.

1.17 true

1.18 true

1.19 false

1.20 true

1.21 true

1.22 false

1.23 partner check

1.24 partner check

1.25 partner check

1.26 partner check

1.27 e

1.28 c

1.29 a

1.30 b

1.31 true

1.32 true

1.33 false

1.34 true

1.35 false

1.36 297

1.37 86

1.38 484

1.39 none

1.40 195

1.41 326

1.42 232

1.43 195

1.44 484

1.45 false

1.46 true

1.47 true

1.48 false

1.49 true

1.50 true

1.51 partner check

1.52 teacher check

1.53 d. pray for him

1.54 c. it is hard to love enemies

1.55 b. returning kindness

1.56 let him take your cloak also

1.57 bless them

1.58 do good to them

1.59 pray for them

1.60 - 1.62 Examples:

1.60 He loved His enemies enough to die for their sins. He forgave them and prayed for God to forgive them.

1.61 He loved and taught about Jesus.

1.62 the Holy Spirit

1.63 Across
1. Christians
2. mercy
3. rich
4. leper
5. love
6. show

Down
7. disciples
8. Samaria
9. forgive
10. poor

1.64	teacher check	1.67	false
1.65	partner check	1.68	false
1.66	a. Dorcas making clothing for needy	1.69	true
	b. Jesus feeding five thousand	1.70	true
	c. Jesus dying on the cross for my (our) sins	1.71	true
	d. Jesus weeping over Jerusalem		

SECTION TWO

2.1 partner check

2.2 a. It is written, Man shall not live by bread alone, but by every word that proceedeth out of the mouth of God.

b. and in their hands they shall bear thee up, lest at any time thou dash thy foot against a stone.

c. It is written again, Thou shall not tempt the Lord thy God.

d. All these things will I give thee, if thou wilt fall down and worship me.

e. Get thee hence, Satan, for it is written, Thou shalt worship the Lord thy God and him only shalt thou serve.

2.3 "Whosoever shall smite thee on thy right cheek, turn to him the other also." Matthew 5:39

2.4 "Whatsoever ye do, do it heartily, as to the Lord, and not unto men;" Colossians 3:23

2.5 "Children, obey your parents in all things…" Colossians 3:20

2.6 "Lay not up for yourselves treasures upon earth… for where your treasure is, there will your heart be also." Matthew 6:19-21

2.7 "Thou shalt not bear false witness against thy neighbor." Exodus 20:16

2.8 false

2.9 true

2.10 false

2.11 false

2.12 true

2.13 true

2.14 false

2.15 true

2.16 It is written

2.17 Luke 24:46 and 47 and First Corinthians 15:3 and 4

2.18 Jesus is in heaven.

2.19 He is preparing a place for His people.

2.20 teacher check

2.21 d

2.22 a. 5
b. 1
c. 3
d. 6
e. 4
f. 2

2.23 c, d

2.24 Any order:
a. He was a ruler--a Pharisee
b. He knew the laws of the leaders (Scribes and Pharisees)
c. He knew the Old Testament

2.25 a. Samaritan
b. disliked
c. sinner
d. Pharisee
e. ruler
f. sinner
g. respected

  h. little
  i. publican
  j. disliked
  k. rich
  l. tax collector
  m. sinner
2.26 1. Zacchaeus
    2. Jesus
    3. Stephen
    4. Dorcas
    5. Nicodemus
    6. Stephen
2.27 Savior
2.28 army commander
2.29 Holy Spirit
2.30 pleased
2.31 name
2.32 save
2.33 Any order:
    a. the Bible
    b. God
    c. Jesus Himself
2.34 b, c
2.35 b, c
2.36 a
2.37 partner check
2.38-2.39 Examples:
2.38 People need to know that Jesus
    came to die for their sins. He
    saves them from death.
2.39 He looks at Jesus in us. Jesus
    never sinned. When we "accept
    Jesus," God sees Jesus in us.
2.40 b
2.41 c
2.42 a
2.43 a
2.44 partner check
2.45 everywhere the Lord puts you
2.46 always
2.47 Example:
    No, Jesus had told him he would
    suffer for witnessing.
2.48 Verse 23
    a. in labours more abundant
    b. in stripes above measure

  c. in prisons more frequent
  d. in deaths oft (often left for dead)
Verse 24
thirty-nine stripes five times
Verse 25
  a. beaten with rods three times
  b. stoned
  c. shipwrecked three times
  d. a night and a day in the deep
Verse 26
  a. many journeys
  b. perils of water
  c. perils of robbers
  d. perils by the countrymen
  e. perils by the heathen
  f. perils in the city
  g. perils in the wilderness
  h. perils in the sea
  i. perils among false brethren
Verse 27
  a. tired and in pain
  b. often watching (praying)
  c. hungry and thirsty
     or often fasting, cold and without
     clothing
2.49 everywhere
2.50 a. surprised
    b. Lord
    c. suffer
2.51 a. witnessed
    b. Caesar's
2.52 Rome
2.53 a. sang praises
    b. jailer
    c. church
2.54 Story should include some things
    about talking to him about baseball –
    or giving him a book on baseball to
    show an interest in the neighbor's
    interest
2.55 a. ar' gu ment
    b. be lieve'
    c. con tent'
    d. con' tent
    e. con ver sa' tion
    f. dis ci' ple

g. en' e my

h. ex plain'

i. im por' tant

j. pa' tient ly

k. proph' et

l. pub' li can

m. sec' tion

n. tes' ta ment

2.56 <u>Across</u>

1. glory

2. saved

3. persecute

4. gospel

5. night

<u>Down</u>

1. grace

6. glum

7. redeem

8. sinner

9. Apostle

2.57 true

2.58 true

2.59 false

2.60 false

2.61 false

2.62 true

2.63 false

2.64 true

SECTION ONE

1.1 "…he that hath seen me hath seen the Father; and how sayest thou then, Shew us the Father? Believest thou not that I am in the Father , and the Father in me? the words that I speak unto you I speak not of myself: but the Father that dwelleth in me, he doeth the works."

1.2 Solomon

1.3 king

1.4
   (a) 2:6
   (b) 3:5
   (d) 15:1
   (e) 13:18
   (g) 22:29
   (h) 28:27
   (j) 18:15

1.5
   a. kingdom
   b. greatest
   c. teaching

1.6 joyful

1.7 timeless

1.8 no

1.9 yes

1.10 God is pleased when we seek His knowledge.

1.11 Ask God for knowledge.

1.12 teacher check

1.13 a

1.14 a

1.15 b

1.16 b

1.17 a

1.18 a

1.19 b

1.20 a

1.21 Any order:
   a. promises
   b. commands
   c. principles

1.22 b

1.23 a

1.24 c

1.25 Proverbs 3:5

1.26 Proverbs 2:6

1.27 Colossians 2:3

1.28 Proverbs 3:6

1.29 Proverbs 1:7

1.30 John 13:17

1.31 In all our ways acknowledge Him.

1.32
   a. sin
   b. afraid
   c. love
   d. Jesus
   e. understand

1.33 true

1.34 true

1.35 true

1.36 false

1.37 true

1.38 false

1.39 true

1.40 no

1.41 false

1.42 false

1.43 true

1.44 true

1.45
   a. 6
   b. 1
   c. 3
   d. 7
   e. 4
   f. 2
   g. 5

1.46
   a. all
   b. heaven
   c. earth
   d. thrones
   e. him
   f. for

1.47
   a. Lord
   b. God
   c. made
   d. people
   e. sheep

1.48 God told them what to write.

1.49 to glorify Him

1.50	true		1.62	teacher check
1.51	false		1.63	false
1.52	false		1.64	true
1.53	false		1.65	false
1.54	true		1.66	true
1.55	true		1.67	true
1.56	false		1.68	true
1.57	teacher check		1.69	a. im por tant

1.58 Either order:
   a. to understand Bible–land customs
   b. to learn about the settings for the events of the Bible

1.69 a. im por tant
   b. fer tile
   c. cres cent
   d. moun tains
   e. Bi ble
   f. Ti gris

1.59 customs

1.60 setting

1.61 Tigris
   Jordan
   Euphrates

1.70 a. great
   b. bless
   c. great
   d. blessing

1.71 Abraham

SECTION TWO

2.1 teacher check

2.2 gospel

2.3 a. received
   b. power
   c. sons
   d. God
   e. believe

2.4 geography

2.5 timeless

2.6 proverb

2.7 sin

2.8 Genesis

2.9 knowledge

2.10 Son

2.11 died

2.12 sin

2.13 Jesus

2.14 knew, Son, him, would, do

2.15 There shined round about him a light from heaven.

2.16 He thought they were lying about the Resurrection.

2.17 spoke to him from heaven as a light shined down

2.18 Acts

2.19   a bright light

2.20   a. died
       b. buried
       c. rose
       d. third
       e. scriptures

2.21   true

2.22   false

2.23   true
2.24   true
2.25   true
2.26   false
2.27   a
2.28   a
2.29   b
2.30   b
2.31   a

2.32-2.33 Examples:
2.32   Be good so I will not get into any trouble. Do not join in.

2.33   help her, run errands, play with the baby, or do what she says
2.34   God
2.35   yes
2.36   teacher check
2.37   teacher check
2.38   teacher check
2.39   The Lord is my shepherd.

2.40   a. Lord
       b. shepherd
       c. want
       d. pastures
       e. waters
       f. soul
       g. paths
       h. valley
       i. death
       j. me
       k. staff
       l. table
       m. enemies
       n. head
       o. cup
       p. goodness
       q. mercy
       r. house
       s. ever

2.41   teacher check
2.42   Jesus
2.43   David
2.44   Daniel
2.45   sheep
2.46   Christians
2.47   anoint
2.48   Solomon
2.49   commands

2.50   Aquinas

2.51   Canaan

2.52   Proverb
2.53   Peter
2.54   Paul
2.55   memorizing
2.56   Andrew
2.57   Gospel
2.58   Bible

SECTION THREE

3.1   will
3.2   heart
3.3   mind

3.4   heart
3.5   mind
3.6   will

3.7 believing in Him
3.8 to take for one's own
3.9 God's family
3.10 understanding yourself
3.11 God
3.12 glorify
3.13 Christ which strengtheneth me
3.14 For God so loved the world that he gave His only begotten son; John 3:16
3.15 Thy word is a lamp unto my feet, and a light unto my path; Psalm 119:105

3.16 Know ye that the Lord He is God…; Psalm 100:3

3.17 true
3.18 true
3.19 false
3.20 false
3.21 true
3.22 "Go ye into all the world, and preach the gospel to every creature."

3.23 b
3.24 a
3.25 d
3.26 c
3.27 g
3.28 e
3.29 f
3.30 i
3.31 love to one another
3.32 no
3.33 Examples:
a. The little girl would go to the end of the line and wait her turn.
b. The children should go out one at a time so they will not hurt each other.
3.34 teacher check
3.35 teacher check

SELF TEST 1

1.01 Peter's home town

1.02 a person who follows a leader

1.03 a roll of paper with writing on it
1.04 doing wrong
1.05 the Lamb of God
1.06 take away sin
1.07 Andrew
1.08 new name
1.09 a stone
1.010 men
1.011 forgiveness
1.012 wash his feet
1.013 repented
1.014 feed His sheep
1.015 three
1.016 Peter started to sink when he took his eyes off of Jesus.
1.017 A man owed the king. He didn't have the money to pay his debt. The king forgave him. This man saw a man who owed him a smaller amount of money. He couldn't pay. The first man wouldn't forgive him. This made the king angry.

1.018 We should forgive others because God forgave us far more.
1.019 3,000
1.020 1. Peter found Jesus.
     2. Peter followed Jesus.
     3. Peter fished for men.
     4. Peter fed God's sheep.
1.021 for   give
1.022 wor   ship
1.023 san   dal
1.024 truth   ful
1.025 af   ter
1.026 won   der
1.027 fol   low
1.028 mean   while
1.029 breath   less
1.030 al   though
1.031 fif   ty
1.032 win   dow
1.033 ser   mon
1.034 ques   tion
1.035 per   son

SELF TEST 2

2.01   twelve

2.02   enemies

2.03   sins

2.04   doers

2.05   ruler of the Jews

2.06   *Sin* means *doing wrong* .

2.07   Death is the result of sin.

2.08   The children of Israel were bitten by serpents. God told Moses to make a serpent and put it on a pole. Those who looked lived.

2.09   Either order:
   a.   forgives
   b.   cleanses

2.010 tell God about your sin

2.011 Jesus wanted Peter to love Him and to feed His lambs and sheep.

2.012 Either order:
   a.   obey God
   b.   confess sin

2.013 Others will know you are a follower of Jesus if you love other people.

2.014 He took his eyes off of Jesus.

2.015 Any five; any order:
   a.   love
   b.   joy
   c.   peace
   d.   long-suffering
   e.   faith
      or gentleness, goodness, meekness, temperance

2.016 Patience

2.017 completed   completing

2.018 loved   loving

2.019 gave   giving

2.020 deceived   deceiving

2.021 produced   producing

2.022 came   coming

SELF TEST 1

1.01   b.   six days
1.02   c.   God
1.03   b.   Genesis
1.04   c.   a world that God planned
            and created in an orderly way.
1.05   a.   They still have much to
            learn.
1.06   b.   dust
1.07   c.   because He knows our needs.
1.08   b.   a treasure
1.09   b.   righteousness
1.010 c.   day and night
1.011 c
1.012 f
1.013 b
1.014 g
1.015 e
1.016 d
1.017 a
1.018 ~~luck~~   God
1.019 ~~worked~~   rested
1.020 ~~woman~~   man   (or)   ~~dust~~   man
1.021 ~~angels~~   stars
1.022 ~~some~~   all
1.023 ~~eat~~   worry
1.024 ~~Raiment~~   Righteousness
1.025 ~~after~~   before

1.026   Example:
        God made day and night and the
        firmament. God separated water
        from land. He made plant life.
        He made the sun, moon, and the
        stars. God made birds and
        animals and people.
1.027   "For by him were all things
        created, that are in heaven,
        and that are in earth, visible
        and invisible, whether they
        be thrones, or dominions, or
        principalities, or powers: all things
        were created by him, and for him:"
1.028   Example:
        Jesus said God knows man's needs.
        He said God takes care of all
        creatures including birds and
        flowers. We are not to worry.
1.029   Example:
        God made me. God loves me.
        God knows everything. God cares.
1.030   Example:
        I pray each day. I read my Bible.
        I am a Christian.

SELF TEST 2

2.01   b.   learn more of God
2.02   c.   is a way to show love for God.
2.03   b.   covers every person,
            subject, situation
2.04   c.   loving Him and His righteousness
2.05   b.   to tell people of God and Jesus

2.06   a.   praying for us
2.07   c.   protection
2.08   b.   on the sixth day
2.09   c.   that God is interested in all
            their needs

2.010 a. when you accept Jesus as your
          Savior
2.011 a. thankful
2.012 b. live righteous lives
2.013 b. over many years
2.014 a. daily
2.015 b. God's Holy Word
2.016 a. are one God
2.017 true
2.018 false
2.019 true
2.020 true
2.021 true
2.022 false
2.023 true
2.024 false

2.025 true
2.026 God
2.027 dust
2.028 righteousness
2.029 Bible
2.030 Jesus
2.031 prayer
2.032 Any order:
       By studying the Bible, by praying,
       through the Holy Spirit, and by
       knowing Jesus.
2.033 Any order:
       By helping me understand the Bible,
       by giving me peace and joy, and by
       taking my prayers to God.

SELF TEST 3

3.01 b. Jesus
3.02 b. chastisement
3.03 b. salvation
3.04 c. people
3.05 a. disciplines us
3.06 b. sin
3.07 b. often
3.08 a. be our Savior
3.09 c. the woman
3.010 b. have all sinned
3.011 true
3.012 true
3.013 false
3.014 true

3.015 true
3.016 false
3.017 false
3.018 true
3.019 false
3.020 false
3.021 ~~men~~   God
3.022 ~~unbelievers~~ believers
3.023 ~~heavens~~   world
3.024 ~~some~~   all
3.025 ~~joy~~   sin
3.026 Example:
       God expects a person to obey God's
       laws and to try to please God.

3.027 Example:
He wants us to correct our mistakes.
He wants us to be better. He
disciplines us because He loves us.

3.028 Any order:
We are to live (or walk) worthy of
the Lord.
We are to be fruitful in every
good work.
We are to increase in the knowledge
of God.

3.029 Examples:
God knows everything.
God knows what is best for us.
God knows our future.

3.030 Any order:
Prays for you
Gives you heavenly thoughts and desires
Helps you understand the Bible

3.031 Example:
He knows we want to be good and
correct our mistakes so He sent Jesus to
die for our sins. He knows what is best
for us, so He disciplines us. Everything
He knows is for our benefit. He
teaches us.

3.032 Example:
So we may know Him, may know of
Hisknowledge, and may discover God's
plan for us.

SELF TEST 4

4.01   b. God
4.02   c. God
4.03   b. wisely
4.04   a. first in our lives
4.05   a. talents
4.06   a. in six days
4.07   b. man
4.08   c. a sense of wonder
4.09   b. God
4.010 a. important
4.011 c. asked God for wisdom
4.012 b. have sinned and have done
            unkind things
4.013 b. the fear of the Lord
4.014 b. be your Savior
4.015 c. happy
4.016 b. when we are young
4.017 b. wrong
4.018 soul
4.019 Bible

4.020 abilities (or talents)
4.021 children
4.022 young
4.023 true
4.024 false
4.025 true
4.026 true
4.027 false
4.028 false
4.029 false
4.030 Examples: He knows what I will
       be when I grow up. I will use
       the talents and abilities He
       has given me. He will let me
       know what His plan is.
4.031 Examples: The Bible tells us.
       He gave His only Son for us. He
       uses His knowledge for our good.
4.032 Jesus died for our sins and
       became our sacrifice.

SELF TEST 1

1.01	c		1.014	5
1.02	f		1.015	4
1.03	d		1.016	2
1.04	e		1.017	a
1.05	h		1.018	b
1.06	a		1.019	b
1.07	g		1.020	a
1.08	b		1.021	c
1.09	j		1.022	c
1.010	i		1.023	c
1.011	3		1.024	a
1.012	6		1.025	c
1.013	1			

SELF TEST 2

2.01	e		2.016	a
2.02	c		2.017	b
2.03	d		2.018	c
2.04	b		2.019	3
2.05	f		2.020	2
2.06	g		2.021	4
2.07	a		2.022	1
2.08	h		2.023	5
2.09	c		2.024	true
2.010	c		2.025	false
2.011	b		2.026	true
2.012	c		2.027	true
2.013	a		2.028	false
2.014	b		2.029	true
2.015	b			

SELF TEST 3

3.01	c	3.019	Paul
3.02	e	3.020	rabbi
3.03	h	3.021	missionary
3.04	f	3.022	Holy Spirit
3.05	b	3.023	shipwrecked
3.06	d	3.024	a. Romans
3.07	a		b. 1 Corinthians
3.08	g		c. 2 Corinthians
3.09	tentmaker		d. Galatians
3.010	synagogue		e. Ephesians
3.011	Pharisees		f. Philippians
3.012	Sadducees		g. Colossians
3.013	Christians		h. 1 Thessalonians
3.014	robes		i. 2 Thessalonians
3.015	light		j. 1 Timothy
3.016	voice		k. 2 Timothy
3.017	blind		l. Titus
3.018	basket		m. Philemon

SELF TEST 1

1.01	h		1.018	true
1.02	j		1.019	false
1.03	f		1.020	false
1.04	g		1.021	c
1.05	c		1.022	a
1.06	i		1.023	c
1.07	a		1.024	a
1.08	d		1.025	b
1.09	b		1.026	c
1.010	e		1.027	a
1.011	true		1.028	b
1.012	true		1.029	b
1.013	false		1.030	A
1.014	true		1.031	C
1.015	true		1.032	B
1.016	true		1.033	A
1.017	false		1.034	C
			1.035	B

1.036 Example:
To receive God's promises you
must obey Him.

SELF TEST 2

2.01	b	2.013	b	2.025	false
2.02	c	2.014	d	2.026	true
2.03	b	2.015	true	2.027	true
2.04	c	2.016	true	2.028	a. word
2.05	c	2.017	true		b. feet
2.06	a	2.018	false		c. path
2.07	a	2.019	false	2.029	a. love
2.08	c	2.020	true		b. thyself
2.09	b	2.021	true	2.030	a. Believe
2.010	c	2.022	false		b. Lord
2.011	a	2.023	true		c. saved
2.012	e	2.024	false		

SELF TEST 3

3.01	d	3.014	true	3.027	Jesus
3.02	b	3.015	false	3.028	message
3.03	a	3.016	tempers	3.029	a
3.04	f	3.017	honeycomb	3.030	b
3.05	g	3.018	poor	3.031	b
3.06	e	3.019	advice	3.032	a
3.07	c	3.020	everyone	3.033	b
3.08	true	3.021	God	3.034	b
3.09	true	3.022	wise	3.035	a
3.010	true	3.023	Dwight Moody	3.036	a
3.011	false	3.024	timeless		
3.012	true	3.025	morning		
3.013	false	3.026	heart		

SELF TEST 1

1.01   i

1.02   b

1.03   e

1.04   j

1.05   f

1.06   d

1.07   a

1.08   c

1.09   h

1.010 David

1.011 the Lord Jesus

1.012 Good Shepherd

1.013 grass and water

1.014 God's Word

1.015 staff

1.016 wild animals

1.017 oil

1.018 water

1.019 a. leads his sheep

1.020 b. put back

1.021 a. right paths

1.022 a. kindness when we do not deserve it

1.023 b. heaven

1.024 b. comfort the sheep

1.025 a. put oil on

1.026 true

1.027 false

1.028 false

1.029 true

1.030 true

1.031 true

1.032 false

1.033 false

1.034 true

1.035 true

1.036 Jesus called Himself the Good Shepherd because He thinks of His disciples and believers as sheep who need Him. Jesus wants to lead, take care, and love His sheep. Jesus wants His sheep to depend upon Him for guiding.

SELF TEST 2

2.01   d

2.02   e

2.03   b

2.04   c

2.05   f

2.06   counted

2.07   God

2.08   Saul

2.09   slingshot

2.010 shepherd

2.011 still waters
2.012 evil
2.013 house of the Lord
2.014 anointed
2.015 Israel
2.016 Good Shepherd
2.017 mercy
2.018 heaven
2.019 boys
2.020 psalms
2.021 false
2.022 true
2.023 false
2.024 false
2.025 true
2.026 false
2.027 true
2.028 true
2.029 false
2.030 true

2.031 Example:
God used David to comfort King Saul with music. God used David to kill Goliath, the enemy of Israel.
2.032 Example:
David did not use armor. David took only his stick and his slingshot with him. David told Goliath he was trusting in God.
2.033 Example:
David took such good care of them. He knew each sheep by name. He protected them.
2.034 Example:
Jesus takes care of me. He knows my needs.

SELF TEST 3

3.01 a. had an excellent spirit
  c. was honest
  d. prayed three times a day
  f. trusted in the Lord
3.02 a. was a shepherd
  c. killed a lion
  d. sang beautiful songs
  f. trusted in the Lord
3.03 a. is the Good Shepherd
  b. knows us by name
  d. chose us and paid for us with His life
  f. wants to lead us
3.04 j
3.05 e
3.06 h
3.07 g
3.08 i
3.09 d

3.010 b
3.011 a
3.012 k
3.013 f
3.014 false
3.015 true
3.016 false
3.017 false
3.018 false
3.019 true
3.020 false
3.021 true
3.022 God
3.023 shepherd
3.024 jealous
3.025 lie
3.026 psalms
3.027 death

SELF TEST 1

1.01	g		1.019	no
1.02	j		1.020	no
1.03	b		1.021	yes
1.04	i		1.022	yes
1.05	f		1.023	yes
1.06	d		1.024	yes
1.07	h		1.025	yes
1.08	e		1.026	no
1.09	a		1.027	yes
1.010	2		1.028	no
	3			
	1		1.029	yes

1.011 1
       2
       3

1.012 children
1.013 people

1.014 sins
1.015 God

1.016 heaven

1.017 Savior

1.018 hurt

1.030 We can see things moved by the wind. We can feel the wind on our faces.

1.031 We can know God exists by what He does.

1.032 Jesus came to earth to be the Jewish Savior. Jesus came to be the Savior from sin for all people.

1.033 a. God promised to give Abram the lands of Canaan.
       b. God promised to give Abram many children.
       or God promised to make of Abram a great nation.

SELF TEST 2

2.01	a. God	2.015	b
	b. made	2.016	a
	c. people	2.017	a
		2.018	b
2.02	a. praise	2.019	b
	b. made	2.020	b
	c. works	2.021	a

2.03 children   2.022 a

2.04 Savior   2.023 b

2.05 people   2.024 b

2.06 Jews, or His people   2.025 Example:

2.07 heaven

2.08 true

2.09 true

2.010 false

2.011 true

2.012 false

2.013 b

2.014 a

2.025 Example:
I can know that God exists by
looking at the world He created.
I know He exists by the things He
does.

2.026 Examples:
a. Thomas Aquinas was a religious
thinker who wrote laws or
arguments to prove God exists.
b. Thomas Aquinas lived long ago.

SELF TEST 3

3.01	sins	3.011	true
3.02	Jesus	3.012	true
3.03	heaven	3.013	true
3.04	body	3.014	true
3.05	Bible	3.015	false
3.06	forty	3.016	true
3.07	Lord	3.017	false
3.08	name	3.018	false
3.09	friar	3.019	false
3.010	fact	3.020	true

3.021 true

3.022 b

3.023 a

3.024 c

3.025 b

3.026 c

3.027 c

3.028 a

3.029 c

3.030 c

3.031 b

3.032 a

3.033 Any order:
a. The earth is round
b. Snowfall is valuable.
c. Lightning is an important part of rainfall.
or Animals will bear only their own kind.

3.034 Jesus came to be the Savior from sin. He came to save the Jewish people.

3.035 I should read the Bible because God wants me to read it. I can learn God's plan for my life.

SELF TEST 1

1.01   f

1.02   k

1.03   b

1.04   h

1.05   j

1.06   c

1.07   d

1.08   e

1.09   g

1.010   a

1.011   b

1.012   a

1.013   a

1.014   b

1.015   b

1.016   b

1.017   d

1.018   f

1.019   a

1.020   c

1.021   ideas or inventions and ideas

1.022   the rich soil from the many rivers

1.023   minerals that are washed into it by the Jordan River

1.024   grow food, travel, find water

1.025   of many kinds of land forms and different climates

1.026   false

1.027   true

1.028   true

1.029   true

1.030   false

1.031   true

1.032   false

1.033   false

1.034   true

1.035   true

1.036   Example:
to gain a better understanding of the Bible land customs and to learn the setting of the events recorded in the Bible

1.037   Example:
from the cold foothills of Mount Hermon to below sea level at Sea of Galilee and dropping through farmlands to the desert around the Dead Sea

1.038   Examples; any order:
a. agriculture
b. domestication of animals
c. systems of law and government

SELF TEST 2

2.01	true	2.028	b
2.02	true	2.029	a
2.03	false	2.030	c
2.04	false	2.031	b
2.05	false	2.032	c
2.06	true	2.033	a
2.07	true	2.034	c
2.08	false	2.035	d
2.09	true	2.036	Ur
2.010	false	2.037	Haran
2.011	f	2.038	Padan-aram
2.012	h	2.039	Example:

2.013   n

2.039   Example:
Sheep were raised for their skins, wool, and meat. Goats were raised for their skins, meat, and milk. These animals could be moved easily from place to place.

2.014   k

2.015   m

2.040   Example:
a. The former rains come in fall. The latter rains come in spring.
b. The former rains were needed when the ground was plowed and the grain was sown. The latter rains were needed to make grain grow for harvesting.

2.016   c

2.017   o

2.018   a

2.019   d

2.041   "And I will make of thee a great nation, and I will bless thee, and make thy name great; and thou shalt be a blessing."

2.020   g

2.021   b

2.042   Any order:
Tigris, Euphrates, Jordan

2.022   i

2.043   Example:
It is the fertile, well-watered area.

2.023   p

2.024   e

2.025   j

2.026   c

2.027   c

SELF TEST 1

1.01	true	1.021	a. He hates it.
1.02	false	1.022	b. Matthew 10:31
1.03	true	1.023	c. of who they are and what they have
1.04	false	1.024	b. love and obedience
1.05	false	1.025	b. the dust of the earth
1.06	true	1.026	They are God's Word – they tell us what God wants us to know and do.
1.07	false	1.027	God breathed into him
1.08	false	1.028	fable
1.09	false	1.029	glory
1.010	true	1.030	God
1.011	d	1.031	A parable is a short story that teaches a lesson. It does not use real people.
1.012	g		
1.013	i	1.032	A fable is a make-believe story that has a moral. A fable has animals in it.
1.014	a		
1.015	j	1.033	I am important to God because God made me. I am very special.
1.016	b		
1.017	f	1.034	He left heaven. He loved poor people He called sinners His friends. He suffered and died for us.
1.018	k		
1.019	e		
1.020	c		

SELF TEST 2

2.01	h	2.06	b
2.02	e	2.07	c
2.03	j	2.08	f
2.04	i	2.09	d
2.05	a	2.010	g

2.011 false
2.012 false
2.013 true
2.014 true
2.015 true
2.016 false
2.017 false
2.018 true
2.019 true
2.020 false

2.021 c
2.022 a
2.023 c
2.024 a
2.025 c

2.026 glory
2.027 wonderful
2.028 Himself

2.029 good
2.030 God
2.031 will
2.032 Any order:
   a. will
   b. mind
   c. heart
2.033 adopt
2.034 Any order:
   a. Father
   b. Creator
   c. Lord
2.035 die
2.036 Example:
   When we accept God's son as our
   Savior we become God's child
   and a part of God's family.

SELF TEST 3

3.01 c
3.02 a
3.03 d
3.04 b
3.05 f

3.06 true
3.07 false
3.08 false
3.09 true
3.010 false
3.011 false
3.012 false
3.013 true
3.014 false
3.015 false

3.016 b. the dust of the earth
3.017 a. stone
3.018 b. Philistine
3.019 c. giant
3.020 a. child
3.021 b. glory
3.022 c. forever
3.023 a. He made you
3.024 b. trust Jesus

Bible 408 Self Test Key

3.025 c. knowing and respecting God

3.026 themselves

3.027 sin

3.028 image

3.029 parables

3.030 God

3.031 glory

3.032 publican

3.033 heart

3.034 fear

3.035 grow

3.036 Example:
   Because God made me wonderfully
   and He loves me. God wants the
   very best for me. He gives me
   the good gifts that I need.

121

SELF TEST 1

1.01	commandments	1.018	g
1.02	mirror	1.019	d
1.03	doers	1.020	c
1.04	sin	1.021	false
1.05	thank	1.022	false
1.06	Holy Spirit	1.023	true
1.07	witness	1.024	false
1.08	disciples	1.025	true
1.09	obey	1.026	true
1.010	persecuting	1.027	false
1.011	i	1.028	true
1.012	f	1.029	true
1.013	h	1.030	false
1.014	a	1.031	false
1.015	b	1.032	ye love me, keep my commandments
1.016	k	1.033	every thing give thanks, for this is the will of God in Christ Jesus concerning you
1.017	e		

SELF TEST 2

2.01	true	2.06	true
2.02	true	2.07	true
2.03	true	2.08	false
2.04	true	2.09	true
2.05	false	2.010	false

2.011 h

2.012 n

2.013 j

2.014 m

2.015 g

2.016 p

2.017 d

2.018 k

2.019 c

2.020 b

2.021 e

2.022 f

2.023 o

2.024 a

2.025 i

2.026 l

2.027 a. the water Jesus could give her

2.028 d. many times

2.029 c. Nicodemus

2.030 a. Paul's guard

2.031 b. listen to the other person

2.032 c. Satan tempted Him

2.033 b. Matthew

2.034 c. hanged

2.035 b. Samaritans

2.036 c. a Roman

2.037 a. preach without ceasing

2.038 b. change people's hearts

2.039 a. I live ye
       b. John

2.040 a. His only begotten Son, that whosoever believeth in Him should not perish, but have everlasting life.
       b. 3:16

2.041 a. heart, that I might not sin against Thee
       b. Psalm

2.042 a. that ye are my
       b. ye have love one to another
       c. John

SELF TEST 1

1.01	b	1.017	false
1.02	f	1.018	true
1.03	c	1.019	true
1.04	h	1.020	true
1.05	d	1.021	a. spiritual
1.06	g		b. physical
1.07	b	1.022	Scripture
1.08	c	1.023	God
1.09	a	1.024	sin
1.010	a	1.025	Genesis
1.011	c	1.026	knowledge
1.012	b	1.027	Example:
1.013	c		Proverbs 2:6 For the Lord giveth
1.014	c		wisdom: out of his mouth cometh
1.015	a		knowledge and understanding.
1.016	false		

SELF TEST 2

2.01	3	2.013	i
2.02	2	2.014	b
2.03	6	2.015	d
2.04	1	2.016	a
2.05	5	2.017	a
2.06	4	2.018	b
2.07	a. want	2.019	c
	b. pastures		
	c. waters	2.020	a
	d. soul		
	e. righteousness	2.021	b
	f. death		
	g. staff	2.022	c
	h. table		
	i. oil	2.023	c
	j. cup		
	k. mercy	2.024	a
2.08	c	2.025	c
2.09	e	2.026	true
2.010	g	2.027	false
2.011	h	2.028	false
2.012	f	2.029	true

2.030 true

2.031 false

2.032 false

2.033 true

SELF TEST 3

3.01 will

3.02 glorify

3.03 Christ

3.04 God

3.05 yourself

3.06 Epistles

3.07 Gospel

3.08 Bible

3.09 a

3.010 c

3.011 b

3.012 a

3.013 c

3.014 b

3.015 b

3.016 false

3.017 true

3.018 false

3.019 true

3.020 false

3.021 false

3.022 true

3.023 false

3.024 true

3.025 d

3.026 a

3.027 c

3.028 e

3.029 f

3.030 b

3.031 g

3.032 people and the sheep of His pasture

3.033 believe on His name

3.034 dwell in the house of the Lord for ever

3.035 preach the gospel to every creature

Bible 400 Self Test Key

Bible 401
LIFEPAC TEST

1.	g	21.	a follower of a leader like Jesus
2.	e	22.	doing wrong
3.	i	23.	he took his eyes off Jesus
4.	j	24.	cleansed or forgiven
5.	d	25.	ruler of the Jews
6.	c	26.	doers
7.	f	27.	confess
8.	h	28.	forgive
9.	a	29.	pray
10.	b	30.	everyone
11.	false	31.	a. deceive
12.	true	32.	c. forgiveness
13.	true	33.	b. owed
14.	false	34.	c. forgive
15.	false	35.	b. pray
16.	false	36.	Any four; any order:
17.	true		a. love
18.	true		b. joy
19.	true		c. peace
20.	true		d. long-suffering

36. Any four; any order:
  a. love
  b. joy
  c. peace
  d. long-suffering
     or gentleness, goodness, faith,
     meekness, temperance

37. Galatians 5:22-23

Bible 402
LIFEPAC TEST

1. Jesus
2. the world, earth
3. God
4. Bible
5. man
6. pray
7. Holy Spirit
8. Genesis
9. God's Kingdom and His righteousness
10. sinned
11. God
12. Solomon
13. seventh
14. c
15. e
16. f
17. a
18. d
19. b
20. g
21. a. reading your Bible
    c. living a Christian life
22. b. to teach us
    c. to discipline us
23. a. the world
    b. man
24. a. the good Shepherd
    c. our Savior
25. b. praying for us
    c. living in our hearts
26. a. can be harmful
    b. is not of God
27. a. superior
    b. marvelous
28. a. above all else
    b. as part of our everyday actions
29. a. talking with Him
    b. living obediently to God

Bible 403
LIFEPAC TEST

1. c
2. g
3. a
4. b
5. d
6. e
7. f
8. 3
9. 7
10. 1
11. 5
12. 4
13. 2
14. 6
15. a
16. b
17. b
18. b
19. c
20. a
21. a
22. c

23. true
24. true
25. false
26. false
27. false
28. false
29. true
30. false
31.
    a. Romans
    b. Galatians
    c. Philippians
    d. 2 Thessalonians
    e. Titus

Bible 404
LIFEPAC TEST

1.	false	16.	b
2.	true	17.	b
3.	true	18.	c
4.	true	19.	a
5.	true	20.	a
6.	false	21.	c
7.	false	22.	b
8.	true	23.	c
9.	heart	24.	c
10.	a. spiritual	25.	b
	b. physical	26.	a
11.	Any order:	27.	e
	a. commands	28.	d
	b. promises	29.	teacher check
	c. principles	30.	teacher check
12.	everyone	31.	teacher check
13.	timeless		
14.	restudy		
15.	a		

Bible 405
LIFEPAC TEST

1.	want	16.	e
2.	pastures	17.	a
3.	waters	18.	David
4.	soul	19.	Jesus
5.	righteousness	20.	Goliath
6.	death	21.	King Darius
7.	staff	22.	King Saul
8.	table	23.	Jew
9.	oil	24.	a
10.	cup	25.	b
11.	mercy	26.	a
12.	house	27.	b
13.	23	28.	b
14.	d	29.	a
15.	b		

Bible 406
LIFEPAC TEST

1.	g
2.	b
3.	e
4.	f
5.	h
6.	d
7.	a
8.	c
9.	a
10.	b
11.	c
12.	c
13.	a
14.	a
15.	b
16.	b

17.	true
18.	true
19.	false
20.	true
21.	false
22.	true
23.	true
24.	false
25.	heaven
26.	God
27.	Savior
28.	Bible
29.	he is God: it is he that hath made us, and not we ourselves; we are his people, and the sheep of his pastures
30.	am fearfully and wonderfully made: marvelous are thy works; and that my soul knoweth right well
31.	God is eternal life through Jesus Christ our Lord
32.	become the sons of God, even to them that believe on his name

Bible 407
LIFEPAC TEST

1. true
2. false
3. true
4. false
5. false
6. true
7. false
8. true
9. false
10. true
11. false
12. true
13. false
14. true
15. true
16. slaves
17. Either order:
    a. crossroads of the ancient world
    b. Fertile Crescent
18. Either order:
    a. paintings
    b. buildings
19. Dead Sea
20. Any order:
    a. Mount Sinai
    b. Kadesh-barnea
    c. Mount Nebo
21. k
22. e
23. f

24. h
25. a
26. c
27. d
28. j
29. b
30. g
31. tents
32. flocks and herds
33. terrain
34. Holy
35. Jordan
36. mountains or ridges
37. Dan or Manasseh
38. shepherds or nomads
39. Canaan
40. Mount Nebo
41. Example:
    Lands included in the Fertile Crescent were Canaan, and the area surrounding the Tigris-Euphrates valley. It was called the Fertile Crescent because it was a well-watered area in the middle of desert country. Civilization began in the Fertile Crescent and trade routes ran through it.
42. "And I will make of thee a great nation, and I will bless thee, and make thy name great; and thou shalt be a blessing."

Bible 408
LIFEPAC TEST

1.	h
2.	j
3.	i
4.	b
5.	c
6.	d
7.	a
8.	f
9.	k
10.	e
11.	false
12.	true
13.	false
14.	false
15.	true
16.	true
17.	false
18.	true
19.	false
20.	false
21.	e
22.	f
23.	b
24.	d
25.	c
26.	God

27. Either order:
    a. love
    b. obey
28. Jesus (Christ)
29. others
30. child
31. c. the dust of the earth
32. b. parables
33. b. proud
34. a. fearfully and wonderfully
35. a. justified
36. Example:
    I must invite Jesus, God's Son, into my
    life and ask Him to forgive my sins.
    I will be in God's family and God will
    see Jesus when He looks at me.

Bible 409
LIFEPAC TEST

1. false
2. true
3. false
4. false
5. true
6. true
7. true
8. false
9. false
10. true
11. false
12. false
13. true
14. true
15. true
16. true
17. j
18. m
19. f
20. k
21. o
22. b
23. l
24. a
25. d
26. e
27. c
28. g
29. i
30. n
31. h
32. p
33. Satan
34. 1 Corinthians 15:3–4
35. John the Baptist
36. sacrifice
37. Psalm 119:11
38. Any order:
   a. the Bible
   b. God
   c. Jesus
39. quoting the Bible
40. Samaritan
41. "If ye love me, keep my commandments."
42. "By this shall all men know that ye are my disciples, if ye have love one to another."
43. "In everything give thanks, for this is the will of God in Christ Jesus concerning you."

Bible 410
LIFEPAC TEST

1. c
2. a
3. b
4. g
5. d
6. e
7. true
8. false
9. false
10. false
11. true
12. true
13. true
14. true
15. true
16. false
17. false
18. true
19. a. Canaan
20. b. the human body
21. c. sins
22. a. Solomon
23. c. happy
24. b. Genesis
25. a. reading the Bible
26. b. David
27. God

28. Bible
29. a. spiritual
    b. physical
30. commands
31. restudy
32. Jesus
33. Epistles
34. Psalm 23
35. Philippians 4:13
36. we are His people, and the sheep of His pasture
37. into all the world, and preach the gospel to every creature

1. b
2. j
3. f
4. k
5. d
6. e
7. i
8. h
9. c
10. a
11. Example:
    Faith is belief or trust.
12. Example:
    We should be sorry about our sins and confess our sins to God.
13. true
14. false
15. true
16. true
17. true
18. false
19. false
20. true
21. false
22. true
23. b. Lamb of God
24. c. men
25. a. feet
26. b. Peter
27. c. disciple
28. a. even our enemies
29. repents
30. forgiveness
31. Word
32. pray
33. brother
34. sheep (lambs)
35. obey
36. forgive

1. true
2. true
3. true
4. false
5. true
6. false
7. false
8. true
9. true
10. false
11. a. all ways
12. b. the Bible
13. b. cares about all their needs
14. a. trying to do the ways of God
15. b. star study
16. e
17. h
18. j
19. b
20. a
21. i
22. k
23. d
24. f
25. g
26. days
27. Genesis
28. dust
29. seventh day
30. *live*
31. Holy Spirit
32. body
33. Son
34. wisdom
35. fear of the Lord

1.   d
2.   g
3.   e
4.   b
5.   c
6.   f
7.   a
8.   3
9.   5
10.   1
11.   6
12.   2
13.   4
14.   7
15.   c
16.   a
17.   b
18.   a
19.   c
20.   b
21.   b
22.   c
23.   true
24.   true
25.   false
26.   true
27.   false
28.   true
29.   true
30.   false
31.   a. 2 Corinthians
       b. Ephesians
       c. Colossians
       d. Titus
       e. Philemon

1. true
2. true
3. true
4. false
5. true
6. false
7. false
8. false
9. commands
10. Any order:
    a. commands
    b. promises
    c. principle
11. sin
12. everyone
13. heart
14. spiritual
15. memorize
16. copy
17. b. God
18. c. proverb
19. c. Solomon
20. a. happy
21. c. feet
22. c. arguments
23. b. secret
24. a. God
25. b
26. c
27. f
28. a
29. e

30-32 Examples:
30. Proverbs 12:23
    "A prudent man conceals his knowledge but fools proclaim their folly."
31. Proverbs 28:11
    "A rich man is wise in his own eyes, but a poor man who has understanding will find him out."
32. Proverbs 22:9
    "He who has a bountiful eye will be blessed, for he shares his bread with the poor."
33. e
34. c
35. d
36. b
37. a

1. h
2. a
3. f
4. i
5. g
6. c
7. b
8. d
9. j
10. Jesus
11. David
12. Good Shepherd
13. Jew
14. King Saul
15. God
16. Goliath
17. King Darius
18. false
19. true
20. false
21. false
22. false
23. true
24. false
25. false
26. true
27. true
28. b. *put back*
29. b. *rights paths*
30. c. *kindness we do not deserve*
31. a. *rub with oil*
32. a. led his sheep
33. b. heaven
34. b. comfort sheep
35. Psalm
36. Psalms
37. lions' den
38. David
39. leads
40. Jesus

1. true
2. false
3. true
4. true
5. false
6. b. made
7. c. blood
8. a. eternal life
9. b. our bodies
10. a. worship God
11. God
12. children
13. heaven
14. Bible
15. exists
16. c
17. a
18. b
19. e
20. d
21. "I will praise thee for I am fearfully and wonderfully made: marvellous are thy works; and that my soul knoweth right well."
22. "Know ye that the Lord he is God: it is he that hath made us, and not we ourselves; we are his people, and the sheep of his pasture."
23. "But as many as received him, to them gave he power to become the sons of God, even to them that believe on his name."
24. "For the wages of sin is death; but the gift of God is eternal life through Jesus Christ our Lord."
25. God promised Abram that He would make a great nation of him.
26. God promised to send a Savior to the Jews.
27. We know that God exists because of the things He does.
28. I read to know God's plan for my life.
29. Man's most important need is to know God.

1. New Jersey
2. *customs*
3. Any order:
   a. systems of law and government
   b. agriculture
   c. domestication of animals
4. Any order:
   a. new products
   b. new tools
   c. new ideas
5. Any order:
   a. Tigris
   b. Euphrates
   c. Jordan
6. Dead Sea
7. deserts
8. Dead Sea
9. spring
10. "And I will make of thee a great nation, and I will bless thee, and make thy name great; and thou shalt be a blessing."
11. a.
12. c
13. e
14. f
15. g
16. h
17. b
18. i
19. j
20. d
21. traveled around to find food and good places to graze his animals.
22. Tigris (or Euphrates or Jordan)
23. wilderness
24. build-up of minerals washed down by the rivers
25. customs
26. Holy
27. *Prince or Soldier of God*
28. earth (dirt)
29. height
30. fertile

1. f
2. c
3. g
4. d
5. b
6. j
7. k
8. e
9. h
10. l
11. a. story with a lesson
12. b. fables
13. c. the first five books of the Bible
14. a. in God's image
15. b. and on earth
16. c. take as your own child
17. a. no beginning nor end
18. c. love Him and all people
19. a. David's son
20. a. sin
21. "But the very hairs of your head are all numbered. Fear ye not therefore, ye are of more value than many sparrows."

22. "Know ye that the Lord he is God: it is he that hath made us and not we ourselves; we are his people and the sheep of his pasture."
23. "I will praise thee; for I am fearfully and wonderfully made: marvellous are thy works; and that my soul knoweth right well."
24. "For every one that asketh receiveth; and he that seeketh findeth; and to him who knocketh it shall be opened."
25. true
26. true
27. false
28. false
29. true
30. true
31. false
32. true
33. false
34. true

1. true
2. false
3. true
4. true
5. false
6. false
7. false
8. true
9. false
10. true
11. k
12. j
13. l
14. a
15. n
16. b
17. c
18. i
19. d
20. g
21. m
22. e
23. Any order:
   a. a. kind acts
   b. b. telling of Jesus
   c. d. guarding your tongue
24. Any order:
   a. a. keeping His commandments
   b. b. loving others
   c. c. witnessing

25. Any order
   a. a. friends
   b. b. disciples
   c. d. doers
26. Any order:
   a. a. do good to that person
   b. c. pray for the person
   c. d. turn the other cheek
27. Any order:
   a. b. Paul
   b. c. the centurion
   c. d. John
28. c. Malachi
29. b. Matthew
30. c. James 3:10
31. b. Exodus 20:3
32. b. the ones who believed in Jesus are saved
33. d. it is God's Word
34. c. God's message
35. commandments
36. save
37. churches
38. prison
39. tongue
40. Jesus or the death of Jesus or the coming of Jesus
41. brothers
42. witness
43. *Savior*

1.	true	26.	e
2.	false	27.	Epistles
3.	false	28.	Jesus
4.	false	29.	restudy
5.	true	30.	commands
6.	true	31.	knowledge
7.	true	32.	God
8.	true	33.	spiritual
9.	true	34.	knowledge
10.	true	35.	shall follow me all the days of my life: and I will dwell in the house of the Lord for ever.
11.	true		
12.	true		
13.	b. David	36.	that whosoever believeth in Him should not perish, but have everlasting life.
14.	a. reading your Bible		
15.	b. Genesis		
16.	c. God	37.	and preach the gospel to every creature.
17.	b. happy		
18.	a. Solomon	38.	we are His people, and the sheep of His pasture.
19.	c. body		
20.	a. the Holy Land		
21.	f		
22.	d		
23.	g		
24.	b		
25.	a		